# HAL KOERNER'S
# FIELD GUIDE TO
# ULTRARUNNING

# HAL KOERNER'S
# FIELD GUIDE TO
# ULTRARUNNING

## TRAINING FOR AN
## **ULTRAMARATHON,**
## FROM 50K TO 100 MILES
## AND BEYOND

## **HAL KOERNER**
### **WITH ADAM W. CHASE**

## FOREWORD BY SCOTT JUREK

VELO
PRESS

Boulder, Colorado

*For my family and my wife, Carly.*
*They've been down since day one.*

 velopress®

3002 Sterling Circle, Suite 100
Boulder, Colorado 80301-2338 USA
(303) 440-0601 · Fax (303) 444-6788 · E-mail velopress@competitorgroup.com

Distributed in the United States and Canada by Ingram Publisher Services

A Cataloging-in-Publication record for this book is available from the Library
of Congress.
ISBN: 978-1-937715-22-9

For information on purchasing VeloPress books, please call (800) 811-4210, ext. 2138,
or visit www.velopress.com.

This paper meets the requirements of ANSI/NISO Z39.48-1992
(Permanence of Paper).

Cover design, interior design, and composition by Andy Omel
Cover photograph by Tim Kemple
Back cover photograph by Brad Kaminsky

Text set in Prensa Light

14   15   16 / 10   9   8   7   6   5   4   3   2   1

# CONTENTS

# 4. GEAR

## 5. MAINTENANCE, SELF-CARE, AND FIRST AID

# WRITER'S NOTE

I WILL NEVER FORGET THE DAY. I DOUBT HAL REMEMBERS IT, but for me, it is an indelible moment. We were racing an early-season 50K in Chatfield State Park, southwest of Denver, Colorado, when Hal came up on me at about the 30-kilometer mark. In his cool-as-a-cucumber, affable way, he passed by me and encouraged me along. I was able to stay with him for a while, and we chatted about his plans for the season. Then he strode away at a pace I could no longer sustain.

I've been passed by many a runner since then, but this was a decade ago, when it didn't happen very often. And it had never happened before with this friendly, respectful, excited young guy who had obvious signs of talent and longevity in the growing sport of ultrarunning. Yet it didn't bother me in the slightest. In fact, as this running phenom pulled away, I remember smiling to myself, feeling as though in some small way I was symbolically passing the torch to the next generation of impassioned ultrarunners. Later, I recall sharing this notion with Hal, telling him that I saw him as carrying the torch for the future of ultrarunning. From the perspective of more than 10 years in the rearview mirror, it turns out I was right on target. Hal has indeed been a primary author in writing the future of this emerging discipline.

Six years after that Chatfield race, after Hal had gone on to win some of the biggest races in the sport, I wrote a story for *Running Times* magazine about Ashland, Oregon, the "new Mecca of ultra-distance running." To get the whole story, I traveled there hoping to get a feeling for what this place was all about. I basked in the warmth of the Rogue Valley Runners, which quickly became apparent to me was better known as "the community that Hal built." While many of the best ultrarunners had moved there to train on the area's soft mountain trails, it was Hal himself—his depth of knowledge, kind words of encouragement, easygoing demeanor, and infectious smile and laughter—who had really drawn the outstanding crowd of young ultrarunners to Ashland. What a treat it was to run and hang with that pack, savoring the friendly banter and humor that Hal kindled, stoked, and shared in.

With this guide, things have come full circle, with Hal sharing his experience and stories with yet a new generation of ultrarunners. My hope is that the text flows like a conversation you'd have with Hal during a long training run or if you stopped in and asked him a question at his Ashland running store. Hal has so many rich stories and lessons to impart to those already in, new to, or aspiring to be in our sport, and I've relished the opportunity to get to know him even better, and on a new level, through this effort. He (quite literally) makes a fast friend.

*—Adam W. Chase*

# FOREWORD BY **SCOTT JUREK**

PART OF WHAT MAKES THE SPORT OF ULTRARUNNING SO alluring is its unique cast of colorful characters and the welcoming sense of community. If it weren't for an eclectic group of influencers and encouraging friends, I don't think I ever would have made that big leap to my first ultramarathon.

Hal Koerner is most definitely one of those characters, and one I'm proud to call a longtime friend. I can't recall whether it was a mountainous 50K in Virginia or a rocky 50-miler in Arizona where I first met Hal. He was a lanky Colorado kid who had his hat pulled down so low you could barely see his chin, but underneath that brim there was always this enormous grin that stayed put, no matter how hard we were hammering up a climb. It was almost unsettling! The other thing about Hal? His undeniable cool. When it came to race mornings, he would barely make it to the start line before the gun went off. However, no matter how late he was, he'd remain utterly unflustered, taking his time to guzzle some coffee and finding his water bottle and gels in the nick of time before springing off to the start with a smile. The thing about Hal is, he never seems to sweat the small stuff—well, except when it comes to picking his race outfit. His race kit was always styled to a T that even the best fashionistas couldn't top!

For 15 years, Hal and I have shared miles on the trail, both racing and training. And despite those many years passing by, not much has changed. Hal is still that same easygoing guy whose smile can set anyone at ease, but yet who can flip the competitive switch and throw down when it matters.

He brings that same laid-back yet competitive style to this guide. Whether you are a newbie ultramathoner or a seasoned veteran, Hal's down-to-earth advice will give you the confidence to get to the finish line or set a personal best. He dispenses hard-earned wisdom on everything from running a downhill properly to wild-animal encounters on the trail. Included are special sections on shaving and, yes, a "Manity Kit"—I'll let Mr. Koerner do the honors of explaining himself on those two points!

The practical, sage instruction in this guide is what helped Hal take the podium in many an ultra, including two straight Western States 100 wins. Hal is hard-core and as "ultra" as it gets, there is no doubt. And yet, while he can rattle off ultra stats like the most studious of ultra geeks, it is his down-home approach and cool head that have served him best in the sport's most grueling and competitive events.

What I enjoy most about Hal is his inviting, fun-loving style, always so welcome on the trail. He brings this trait to his book in spades, all the while serving his guidance straight up like his favorite whiskey. But he gives more than just good advice. Great guidance and best-laid plans can help anyone better understand and participate in our sport, and yet, the truth is, ultramarathoning is too capricious and individual for any rule to be set in stone. It has been said, "Running an ultra is 90 percent mental, and the other 10 percent—that's mental too!" Often it is a strong mind that wins out over strong legs. Hal knows that. He provides you with crucial on-the-ground knowledge in this book, but more important, he'll give you confidence, which may turn out to be your best asset during the inevitable moments of truth in any ultramarathon.

As comprehensively covered as the topics are, I have to admit to being a little disappointed he hasn't included a section on preparing for and recovering from extensive post-race festivities. At these, Hal is the master, as I am sure anyone would agree who has tried to toe the line with him after a race!

I, like Hal, sincerely believe that anyone can run an ultramarathon, and if you follow his advice you won't just complete an ultra, you'll have a lot of fun along the way. Because that's Hal: completely committed to the task at hand, but completely committed, too, to enjoying the journey. I sincerely hope you take that lesson to heart and enjoy your own journey. And in those low moments when it seems impossible, those times that make you wonder if you have any more to give—dig deeper. That's what ultras are all about.

Keep digging deep!

# PREFACE

**I CAN STILL RECALL THE PUNISHING WIND AND THE WHITE-** caps that danced atop the Snake River as I made my way alongside a trough of water raging next to a black strip of road that turned out to be the "easy" miles of the WSU 100K. Looking back on 20 years and some 130 ultras, I find it wonderful and perplexing that it all began in this rugged and desolate place around Pullman, Washington, far removed from just about everyone and everything I knew, which is probably the reason I loved it most.

I had always had a passion for adventure. In my younger, formative years, I played every sport, became an Eagle Scout, dabbled with endurance on the bike—but finally I found the repetition of my two feet could take me places that many my age could not possibly have dreamed. That day in Washington was my inaugural journey. I recall a sense of relief that the towering cedar and taut Douglas fir would let me skate by unseen beneath their generous cover so that

I might not disappoint anyone or be disappointed in myself if I wasn't able to pull this off. Truth is, I was completely and woefully unprepared, but for whatever reason, I was ready to bet the house on this ridiculously long race.

I had absolutely no idea how to train for something like this; in choosing this race, I had all but thrown a blind dart among the dozens of brief classified ads in the back of *UltraRunning* magazine. The description for the WSU 100K was succinct: "Sixty-two miles of mostly paved, rolling countryside that includes a 1,900-foot downhill as well as a 1,700-foot climb on dry, dusty, gravel roads." I supposed this was all I needed to know.

Not quite.

This book, or compendium, if you will, has been gleaned from a lot of sweat and soil, a few masterful moves, a sprinkle of podium pride, and the amusing and maybe not-so-amusing errors and near escapes that have made up two decades of running. In sum, things didn't always go smoothly. But if there were no mistakes, how would we learn? What I want to offer you here is the guide that I wish had accompanied me on my first ultras. While its contents may not dull the ache of weary legs spurred on by a furious, spinning mind during those many miles, I do hope it entertains, teaches, and, most of all, inspires you.

I fell from first place that day in Pullman, right at the 26-mile mark, and then entered into a battle for a step on the podium on that last gradient into town. And although I watched my winning run turn into a stutter and an eventual walk, I have to say that out of my top 10 list, that race remains one of the biggest victories of my life. Sure, I couldn't walk for a few days afterward, and I struggled even to stand up and sit down, but I was hooked. Moments from that day are indelibly seared into my mind, lending further proof that this was truly a life-changing event. When I crossed that finish line, it was one of the first times in my life that I was not questioning my internal compass or wondering what my next move was. That magic effervescence stayed with me and got me out on my feet a second time, and then another, and, my friends, the magic hasn't let up yet.

These pages offer a peek at my own reasons, drive, and motivation that allow me to keep placing one foot in front of the other at moments when every fiber of my being tells me to give it up. You can certainly read this book from cover to cover, but if you prefer, the material is laid out so that it may be quickly scanned, allowing you to pull from the pages what you need in the moment. This book will also offer you a set of tools for your own tinkering, as you prepare to throw caution to the wind and test the bounds of your running potential. My hope is that, after you read it, the voices of self-doubt and anxiety on your personal road to discovery grow a little more diminutive, just like the distance.

# 1
## GETTING
# STARTED

ULTRA, BY ONE DEFINITION, MEANS "EXTREME." AND SO IT
is perhaps not surprising that when people first hear the term
applied to a running race, they imagine that event must be 100
grueling miles or more. While it is true that some ultras are 100
miles, and certainly some are also quite grueling, the fact is, an
ultramarathon is simply any distance beyond the marathon distance, or 26.2 miles. On the flip side, sometimes runners joke about
having done an ultra because they ran to the start line of a marathon from their car or hotel, adding a mile, or ran to the bathroom

when the marathon was over, adding 0.2 miles to their race. So for the jokesters out there, let's be clear that by "ultra," I am referring to the actual race distance. The most common ultramarathon distances are 50K, 50 miles, 100K, 100 miles, and multiday runs.

## WHY RUN AN ULTRA?

Everyone has his or her own reasons, which are as wildly varied and unique as the people who run ultras. For me, part of the appeal has been that ultrarunning takes me places—both within and without—that I didn't know existed. I have had the privilege of running in some of the most beautiful places on earth, from the southeastern Idaho wilderness and the stunning San Juan Mountains of Colorado to the pristine Alaskan interior, the majestic mountains of Europe, and beyond. Ultras have been my excuse to explore places I've never seen and may never have seen if it weren't for running.

Mentally, ultras have the power to transport me to yet a different kind of unique place, one where I feel totally in the present and everything else sort of fades away. That can be hard to do in our daily lives. I always look forward to that feeling and cherish it when it comes.

Another appeal for me is the tremendous satisfaction of doing something that pushes me to my very limits. Generally speaking, life is pretty well managed for many of us, often even dictated to us. We get up in the morning, drive the same road to work, and do our jobs, and things are overall pretty safe, planned, and secure. We know what life looks like; it's predictable. Similarly, we have devices to do many things for us now. But ultras are far, far less predictable, and they are all you: your faculties, your body, your strength, you on the line. There is no faking it. Thus, finishing an ultra brings an enormous feeling of accomplishment.

Then there is the joy of sharing the miles and the journey with like-minded people. Indeed, it was the community I found in ultrarunning that drew me to the sport in the first place. It is one of the few sports where you can toe the line right beside the best and often have the opportunity to chat with the top competitors. The ultra community is growing, yes, but it still has the soul of a small town and is not impersonal, something that other aspects of life can often be. Many ultra races are sprung from the grass roots and have a laid-back feel that is unique in the sport of running. At the end of a race, for example, you may well sit down in the grass and hear someone playing a guitar as you eat fresh-cooked hamburgers or veggie burgers. Runners and supporters will often stick around for hours after the race, even well into the night. The welcoming atmosphere of the ultra extends far beyond the race itself.

Finally, unlike running down a four-lane road in a marathon, with little space and lots of people, in an ultra race you may not see many other people for miles, and those you do see, you get to know pretty well. The trail and the hardships and triumphs of an ultra have a way of fostering relationships. The trail brings you close. In fact, that is how I have made and maintained most of my relationships to this day, even though those friends have also been my direct competition. When you have 20 hours to run with someone, you end up sharing a lot.

## WHO CAN DO AN ULTRA?

You can. Ultras are open for all. You have to train to achieve at least a base level of fitness, and you have to have the desire, but don't let the distance intimidate you. It doesn't take as much as you may

## YOU KNOW YOU ARE **AN ULTRARUNNER IF...**

- You always have at least one missing toenail.
- Your backpack is full of water.
- You use ChapStick anywhere other than on your lips.
- You have a sit-down pizza party at an aid station.
- You immediately look for a bush when the line to the public restroom is long.
- Your run demands both a headlamp and sunglasses.
- You purchase skin lube in the economy size.
- You sign up for a marathon just to get in part of your long run.
- You use more than one pair of shoes for a race.
- You worry about explaining your powders and salt tabs to TSA agents.
- Everything in your pantry is organized in ziplock bags.

think to go from running a few miles to running many. With passion, drive, and smart training, almost anyone can do an ultra. It helps if you have a network of support from folks around you, but the motivation and determination all have to come from you.

Are some people dealt a better hand for executing ultras? Sure. They may have gifts from birth that provide a jump start, physically or mentally. However, that doesn't exclude others. At the highest level of any sport or effort, there are some who are freakishly suited to it, but that certainly should not prohibit anyone else from trying and succeeding.

# TACKLING THE DISTANCE— 50K, 50 MILES TO 100K, AND 100 MILES

As just mentioned, ultra distances are anything over 26.2 miles, and you have several popular distances to choose from. Most people tackling an ultra distance have a marathon or two under their belt, and I would certainly advise it. Is it possible to go from couch to ultra? Well, let's just say I've seen it done but would not recommend it.

The good news is that the base mileage you need when you prepare for a marathon is nearly the amount you'd need for one of the lesser ultra distances. Preparing for an ultra is not so much about miles; it is more mental, deciding which distance you'll tackle and committing to it.

A common path to an ultra looks like this: You do a marathon and then begin to plan out a period of time, say a year, in which you will take logical stepping-stones up in distance, from 50K to 50 miles to 100K and ultimately to 100 miles.

Whichever distance you choose to prepare for, you will need to commit to at least 5 days a week of consistent training for a minimum of 14 weeks. Add in a reasonable 2-week taper, and thus a 16-week training plan can begin any ultra training. Even the shortest ultra is long and taxing, so if you want to finish it and finish it well, you have to put the work in.

## 50K—Steps to Increase the 26.2-Mile Threshold

This distance, which is only 5 miles longer than the marathon distance, demands a similar base mileage. You can successfully prepare for a marathon doing 50 to 90 miles a week. The same is true for a 50K race. So, if you have done a marathon, you will find that training for a 50K demands something similar to what you are used to. However, as you will see in the training plan, the long run may be longer than what you are used to. Thus, perhaps you will be dealing with a less-familiar feeling of being very run-down or of pushing yourself when you have nothing left.

Not only are 50Ks great building blocks for those ultimately shooting for a 100K or 100-mile ultra, but they also serve as "speed training" for seasoned ultrarunners who want to work on faster turnover and run hard throughout the entire distance. And, because the distance is normally covered entirely during the daylight hours, some ultrarunners seek out highly technical, hilly, or otherwise challenging 50K courses.

## 50 Miles to 100K (62 Miles)—
## Time on Feet Becomes Crucial

These races are gateways to the 100-mile ultra, but the 50-miler and 100K are robust runs in and of themselves, and there is no faking the passion and desire for these distances. They will ask for all that you've got, and then some.

The 50-miler creates a real separation from the 50K in terms of both mileage and ultra distinction. You are doubling the marathon distance and, perhaps more significantly, often taking a mental leap into the unknown. This is the distance of most of my favorite races. Where the 100K and 100-miler may loop, double back, or make a patchwork quilt to gather miles, the 50-miler is often a single loop or a point-to-point route, and many runners who are new to ultra-running find the distance manageable. The runner is rewarded with a challenge that is as stimulating mentally as it is physically. That sometimes makes all the difference between competing and a DNF.

While the 50-mile race is common in the United States, the 100K is less so (although participation is increasing now that qualification standards for some of the more popular 100-milers dictate that runners complete a 100K with a qualifying time in order to be eligible to register). However, the 100K is the international standard for the world championship and is a common distance across Europe and in Asia. If you are a runner who loves a destination race, this might be your distance, but be prepared to run some road miles for the effort.

Oddly enough, my very first ultra was a 100K in Washington State. Better-known races Night of Flanders in Belgium and Trailwalker in Hong Kong were my first experiences with this distance internationally. However, my breakthrough race in 2001 was the Catalina 100K, and I have been trying to duplicate that performance year after year at the Miwok 100K, an American standard.

I've found that the 100K rides in the slipstream of the 100-miler. At the equivalent of 62 miles, it pushes you much closer to the 100-mile mark and comes with its own set of difficulties and realities. As you move up from the 50K distance, those 31 additional miles offer a chance for you to experiment with what you are capable of and where your boundaries are. Ironically, although your body will experience more stress than in the 50K and some probable low points, the extra mileage has the benefit of allowing it enough time to actually come back around again and recharge. This can be a very cool feeling, like coming full circle.

In many ways, the 100K is like a tease for the 100-mile distance. And it is more closely related to a 100-mile race than to a 50-miler. Even with a consistent pace, and if things are going well, your 100K race will be 2 to 3 hours longer than your 50-miler, making it a totally different experience. Twelve miles may not sound like much, but at that point in the race, it is long. As far as time, it is another marathon for some runners!

Where a 50-mile race may request it more politely, the 100K will absolutely demand that you learn the ins and outs of your body, and about nutrition for that distance and time, all things being relative (the course, altitude, and weather).

Finally, the 100K race is fantastic training for a 100-miler. But, remember, it takes about 4 to 8 weeks to recover from the effort, so if you are using it as training for a 100-mile race, be sure to factor the recovery time into your calendar.

In terms of base mileage, you will need to bump the weekly total up by adding about 10 miles to both top and bottom, or 60 to 100 miles per week. As you will see in the training plans, I don't advise going crazy with lots of mileage. It's overkill, you run the risk of injury if you bump things up too quickly, and it's hard to recover from high-mileage weeks. I've run a great 100K on 90-mile training weeks. The key is to stay healthy, strong, and consistent. Your long runs need to be run well and after full recovery from the previous long effort.

## 100 Miles—Putting It All Together

Preparing for a 100-mile race means targeting a weekly base of 80 to 110 miles, with a long run of 50 miles. In my own training, my longest training run might be only 30 to 40 miles, however, because I race a lot of 50-mile and longer races in between my 100-milers. And I'd encourage you, too, to put a 50-mile race into your own 100-mile training plan. Besides providing the miles, a race environment offers you experience working through nerves, testing your nutrition, pushing yourself harder than you would otherwise, and encountering and getting through the kinks that present themselves along the way. You will want to place this race strategically within your training. The training plan in this book will indicate where a 50-mile race might fit in nicely.

If you can't find a race that works for you, then you will need to do a 50-miler on your own, not to mention 25-, 30-, and 35-mile runs. Keep in mind that you may need to travel to do really effective distance runs. If you're going to do all the training and work but not even come close to replicating the race itself, then you aren't doing yourself a lot of favors. If, for example, your race has a huge climb, it would be highly beneficial to have done one during a long training run. Likewise, if you envision racing in the heat of the summer in a hot climate or in the wintry wilds of Alaska, then you should be adding those conditions into your training by some means. I would go so far as to say that the requirements of the course should be on your mind daily.

Running at night should be something with which you become very familiar. This is a great time to grab your pacers and pull them into the fold because they will more than likely join you through the nocturnal stage of the race. Getting out the door for a night run when you are dead tired and searching for that second wind will be instrumental in hardening your mind as well as your body. And night running will become more of a routine than a novelty as the mileage increases.

Preparing for a 100-mile race also means practicing even more continual time on your feet, regardless of the miles. Being on your feet for 10 to 12 hours is something you should practice at least once. This will be invaluable to your recovery and endurance strength as well. The long runs in this training plan will give you that ever-so-valuable time on your feet.

## CHOOSING YOUR FIRST RACE

When you are registering for a race, many factors will influence your decision to stay committed to the plan. The preceding section gave you a very broad idea of the time constraints and commitment necessary to pull off an ultra. Take that time element into account as you consider which ultra is best.

For your first ultra, consider finding an event close to home where you can account for most or all of the variables of the course and take advantage of the specificity of your training. Weather, climate, and altitude are all very hard to replicate. For a flatlander living in Iowa, training for the Wasatch Front 100-Mile Endurance Run may be a lot to bite off. By contrast, if you are a Colorado runner, running trails and scaling mountains, this type of training, while awesome, may not translate into the efficiency demanded by the Comrades Marathon, which is 56 miles of rolling pavement in South Africa.

Remember, the learning curve may be a bit steep on the first ultra race you run, so being able to cope and train in familiar surroundings will go a long way toward helping you finish the endeavor. Minimizing extraneous circumstances that have the tendency to trip up the beginning ultrarunner may be the best favor you do for yourself.

If, however, you are set on a race that is much farther afield, so be it. After all, the unknown is part of the adventure, right? But when it comes to training, just know that you will want to get creative and replicate your upcoming race conditions as best you can. The good news is that this creativity can be invigorating and stave off redundancy in your weeks of training. Living in Seattle and training for the Trailwalker 100K in Hong Kong, I incorporated all the steps I could find into my weekly runs in order to syncopate my pace for the rigors of the course's route. While my time was well spent on stairs, I neglected to train for the difference in weather and fell ill to the effects of running in 90-degree temperatures and 100 percent humidity. By mile 20 I was lying perpendicular across the trail like a zombie. As it turned out, perhaps practicing rolling down stairs would have served my training better.

## SETTING A GOAL

Think about either target pace or target time. Look to a friend who has done the distance and whose running you are familiar with for an idea of how fast you can go or how long it might take you. Another idea is to review race results from previous years and choose a midrange finishing time to shoot for. Or, if you are attempting to use the race to qualify for something else, setting a target has already been done for you by the race organization.

While it is important to have a finishing time in mind when you train for a race, it is probably even more important to be flexible about that objective. You will need to adjust it on the fly, especially if the weather or course conditions are less than ideal for running your goal pace. Even if you start out on track to achieve your desired finish, circumstances change quickly during an ultra, and you can suddenly find yourself switching from "I'm going to finish well under my goal!" to "I'll be lucky to even crawl over the finish line." Ultras are lessons in life, and many of the most powerful teaching experiences are gained by dealing well with adversity.

# 2
# TRAINING

**JUST AS A JOURNEY OF A THOUSAND MILES BEGINS WITH THE** first step, your ultra race begins with solid training. To do it right, you'll want to be sure that you approach your training plan with attention to the pace of each session and to integrate runs that allow you to focus on ascending and descending technique so that you feel strong and confident going into the hills. You'll need to know when and how to use speed work, when to ease off, when to go long and how long to go, and when and how to crosstrain or hit the weight room. Whether or not you need a coach is a personal decision.

Regardless, you'll need to know how to integrate tempo runs, rest days, core training, how to mix in road and trail runs and the appropriate mileage progressions, how to stretch, and how to use prep races to peak for your A race. Training for an ultra is a rather involved recipe, but you are the chef, and hopefully a gourmet one at that.

## PACE

Pacing is important in running any distance, but in ultra races it is a different animal altogether. Let's get that clear right from the start. Road marathon courses allow you to figure your splits, with a relatively predictable terrain across a relatively short time frame. Even trail marathons, which can certainly involve climbing and other terrestrial unpredictability, are held across a relatively manageable time frame and distance, allowing more margin for error in a pacing strategy.

To adopt the same pacing strategy as you would for shorter distances and attempt to apply it to the ultra is to set yourself up for disappointment or failure. It is just unrealistic. The majority of 50- or 100-mile courses range up, down, and across wilderness trails and are similar to one another only in their sheer variety. As has often been said of the trail, no two steps are alike. Put it this way: A finishing time in a 100-miler can range anywhere from 13 hours to 3 days.

I am often asked, "Hal, what's your best time?" This isn't a question that can be answered easily, or even correctly. Races are vastly different from one another, and certainly not all finishing times are created equal. I've run races with results that have exceeded all my expectations and of which I am extremely proud, and yet those times are considered slow next to a different race of the same distance.

If you've ever been to Chamonix, France, and tried to circum-navigate Mont Blanc, then you know that a good time for doing so can't be compared to, say, a time for the Angeles Crest 100 or the Arkansas Traveller 100. But remember this: Steve Prefontaine never ran a race for a time; he went out there to win. You may find yourself in that same battle, and your idea of a win may be just to finish, so don't get caught up in relating your time to anyone else's, or even your own prior time on that route. There are so many vari-ables even on the same course from year to year, so keep a level head and put pace in perspective.

So if pacing an ultra is not mainly about numbers or splits, what *is* it about? Pacing in an ultra is about leaving enough in the bank to last you to the end. There is a golden rule of ultra pacing, or at least an old adage: If you think you are starting the race slow, then slow down even more. Adrenaline at the beginning of a race will hype you up, other people around you will hype you up, and you are likely to go out too fast. Crew and family members will build you up at an aid station and release you back into the wild, but that energy rush will fade a few miles later as your pace and energy plummet. You may still feel great at the halfway point, but remem-ber you may have another 12 hours or so to go, depending on the distance you are racing. A big part of completing a successful ultra is learning to discipline yourself to start steady and stick to your plan. That is pacing. Believe me, no matter how slow your pace is, you won't finish a 50- or 100-miler with energy in reserve. And no one will accuse you of not pushing hard enough!

Let's say you have trained to start out running 12-minute miles, and that this has felt comfortable in your training. On race morn-ing, however, you feel great right out of the gate and start off at

11-minute miles. Will you finish the 100 miles more quickly? Mathematically, it would seem that you would, right? However, not only are you unlikely to finish faster than you've trained for, but chances are excellent that you will not make your goal or perhaps will not finish the event at all.

None of us like to slow down, but in an ultra, you can count on it. But even when you're slowing in an event, the right pace assures that you still have gas in the tank not just physically but also mentally. Like any good sports car, you've got to have an internal governor that keeps you from redlining and blowing out your engine, that forces you to stick to a sustainable pace.

This is a good time to rethink pacing. Understand that it is not so much about cadence but, rather, about understanding your body. It is about recognizing your breathing patterns, feeling your body out, and trying to maintain a certain level of comfort across the miles. It is not about numbers alone but about keeping a realistic expectation of what you can do. Staying strong, staying well, staying even, such that at any given moment you have another gear or something in reserve for the long haul: These are the foci during a race.

In an ultra, pacing is certainly a mental game, too. There are going to be more footsteps than you have ever encountered, and it will seem like they will never end. If you can adjust your mental outlook to accept that, you will be in the right headspace. When things got tough, I used to remind myself that I was just so happy not to be sitting in a classroom all day (during my days at college) or behind the wall of a cubicle in a stuffy office (a former job).

I remember running the first few miles of the Angeles Crest 100 with my friend Tommy Nielson, who asked me how I was feeling about the run. "Just running among mountains and trees for a while, a long while," I replied. It was a vague answer and a little bit of an understatement given the miles ahead, but I think you need that appreciation for the little things when the task at hand starts to feel overwhelming.

Practically speaking, through training, you will learn what is a comfortable pace, and discovering that should be among your central goals in training. Comfortable is a good thing. Comfortable preserves your endurance—both physically and mentally—thus allowing you to focus on other key elements that contribute mightily to your success: breathing, hydrating, and nutrition.

Attaining a certain level of comfort on a training run is relatively easy. In a race, which is likely to be double the distance of your longest training run, maintaining that same comfortable pace throughout won't be possible. So when I go out on a training run, I often remind myself, out loud and with a laugh, "I'm *way* ahead of race pace for Western States right now!" Expect that difference on race day. Don't let it disarm you.

The practice of negative splitting does have its place in competitive ultrarunning. Some of the best ultrarunning performances for folks I know came when the runner managed a negative split, running the second half of the race faster than the first half. The practice of negative splitting is something that you can incorporate into your training if you wish. Instead of doing a 30-mile long run where you drag yourself home the last 6 miles, hold back a little during the first half of the run and pace yourself carefully so that you are able to charge those final 6 miles, running them as the fastest part of the whole run. You may even throw in a progression run up to 20 miles, where you steadily step up your pace in 5-mile increments. You will not only realize physiological benefits from this practice but also gain a tremendous psychological advantage, knowing you are capable of pushing hard, even after putting so many miles on your legs.

## TRAIL TECHNIQUE

To best train for an ultra, you should endeavor to get out one to two times a week for specificity training, by which I mean you are out in conditions that are as similar as possible to what you will face on race day. If you will be doing an ultra on the trails (and most do take place on trails), then specificity training means running on trails rather than roads, and on hills or unpredictable terrain rather than flat pavement.

 ## What if **I don't live near trails?**

I didn't peak as a competitive ultrarunner until I moved to Ashland, Oregon, where I had access to trails every day. This consistent running on undulating, unpredictable trails gave an immense boost not just to my skill level but also to my confidence on race day.

Realistically, though, we don't all live next door to trails or beside mountains with gradients you can train on in order to crush you race. And I'm not suggesting you move your house to feed your running habit! I simply advise you to be highly cognizant of the terrain you'll traverse in the race and do your best to replicate it with the real thing, an approximation in your local or area, or even a treadmill.

If all else fails, at least mentally prepare yourself for the racecourse by doing your due diligence with a map. Knowing the profile inside and out—and other specifics of the race—is far better than nothing. After all, running an ultra is largely mental, so never underestimate the value of preparing your mind for the race. I have stayed up many nights poring over Google Earth researching racecourses, planning how to get out of a particular quagmire, or where to rest up for the next one.

You may be a very experienced road runner. However, there is a learning curve to being on the trail. It takes practice to feel comfortable in that element. Uneven ground, soft and shifting terrain, sharp climbs and descents, scrambles, singletrack—these are some of the elements that make trail running unique. Master them through practice.

Your race will benefit from training hours spent getting your body accustomed to using the different muscle groups that trail terrain demands and to the lateral movements that are required on trails. You can also practice navigating the different terrain that is going to come at you on a trail. When you run the Boston Marathon, for example, you know that Heartbreak Hill comes at mile 22, you know exactly what it looks and feels like, and you can prepare yourself for it with hill repeats.

On the trails, finding that kind of absolute consistency is more difficult. Rather, you must always be ready for the unexpected. On the trail, every footfall is different. Nurturing some familiarity with the different types of terrain during your training will help you prepare for almost anything.

## Ascending

Ascending: It seems like you either love it or hate it. Or maybe it is that many runners have a love-hate relationship with it. My favorite thing about the ascent is getting to the top and seeing the view. That is always a great motivator that helps me through the moments when climbing gets really tough.

Mastering ascending is all about form. When you are going uphill, do your best to avoid hunching. Hold your head up and your shoulders back; this helps free up your breathing by keeping your chest open and making the necessary room for your lungs to expand. Also, with your head up, you are able to look where you are going, which is key on a trail where there may be bikers, other runners, tree branches, and numerous potential hazards.

Some studies have shown that the sweet spot for your gaze while running is about 5 yards in front of you. Focusing on that distance allows you to see what is unfolding ahead of you but also allows your brain to pick up your immediate environment peripherally. You can adjust your gaze, depending on the technical nature of the footing, but avoid the temptation to look directly down at your feet; that view can be dizzying, with things moving too fast, and closes off what's ahead or to the side. Instead, check in on your feet periodically and quickly, but then return to your frontward gaze.

Another important aspect to mastering ascending is tied to your footsteps themselves. Having a higher cadence, which means taking smaller, quicker steps, works well on the ascent.

You will target muscle groups differently on the uphill depending on how you run and your exertion level. Speaking for myself, my power comes from my calves and from pushing off through my glutes. Other runners may pull from their abdominal muscles and hip flexors. I try to maximize my power by working through the bigger muscle groups. I also rely on different muscle groups as the trail steepens or changes, allowing for some selective recovery.

For example, if I'm attacking a trail in a more upright position, working through my calves, and then come upon a steeper section, I will switch to a power hike, with my hands on my knees, utilizing my quads more. This allows for the different muscle groups to recover rather than overtaxing just one area. This is similar to a mountain biker who shifts gears, sometimes cranking hard while standing on the pedals, other times spinning in a seated position.

Finally, stay relaxed. Tensing up your muscles and holding your breath won't get you up the hill faster and more likely will make the climb harder. Periodically check in with your breathing and notice any tension in your muscles. As the trail gets more technical, continue to work to find a balance between being focused and staying relaxed. Some accomplished trail and mountain runners gauge their steps per breath and adjust the ratio according to the grade and the trickiness of the footing.

## Power Hiking

Power hiking is a useful tool for ascending. It is particularly great when terrain is uneven and you don't have the ability to maintain an efficient high cadence and still move through rocks easily. It is also useful when a trail is too steep and you need to put your entire foot down for traction, or you are breathing so hard that running

### TREKKING POLES IN ASCENTS

Trekking poles are another tool that many ultrarunners find effective when confronting arduous ascents, especially now that companies are making extremely light yet rigid poles that fold up when not in use. Trekking poles allow you to distribute some of the workload to your upper body, preserving your legs for running later in the race, when you'll need all the energy you have conserved. See Chapter 4 for a more detailed discussion.

becomes less efficient than hiking. The beauty of power hiking is that it keeps you moving; furthermore, it is a strong way to move across mountains.

I admit that I didn't always feel this way about power hiking. I once thought you should run everything. Growing up, I was a great admirer of ultra legend Eric Clifton. He held virtually every 100-mile record for years and was a guy who didn't believe in walking or hiking during a race. I took the same stance for a long while, adhering to the philosophy that changing your form from running to walking to running took more energy, so it was better to just keep on running no matter what. My thoughts on this have evolved, however, and I definitely include power hiking as a tool in the belt. When making that extra effort to run on a climb is more draining than useful, then hiking all or part of that section is a strong choice.

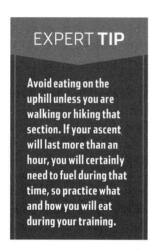

EXPERT **TIP**

Avoid eating on the uphill unless you are walking or hiking that section. If your ascent will last more than an hour, you will certainly need to fuel during that time, so practice what and how you will eat during your training.

## Training for Ascending

Two words: hill work! And to the best of your ability, try to tailor that hill work to the course you are training for and what you will actually be doing. Hill work is great, but not all hill work is created equal. If you know that in the middle of a race you will have a 5-mile climb, and you've been doing 10- to 20-minute climbs in your training, that's not going to be enough to prepare you. Find someplace where you can practice a similar distance uphill. Yes, this means your entire run of the day may be focused completely on the uphill. That's not as fun as going out for a 5-mile easy trail run, but believe me, the work will pay off in your race.

If you're training hard on your uphill, ease up on the downhill, and vice versa. Choose one or the other to run hard, not both. I have a friend who trains for the ascents by going to a ski resort to practice those tough uphill climbs. He runs up a slope, takes the lift back down, runs uphill again, and then repeats. The focus is squarely on uphill training, and he takes it as easy as possible on the way down.

## TECHNIQUE TIPS **FOR THE ASCENT**

**Posture.** Keep your back upright and your gaze directed approximately 5 yards ahead. Keep your head up, even if you must bend forward on the steep grades to put your hands on your knees. Keeping your back straight and your head up allows for better breathing.

**Hips/glutes.** Move your hips forward as if someone is out in front of you, pulling you in with a rope attached to your belt. This keeps your glutes working and allows for better breathing.

**Arms.** Don't forget arm motion! Being strong in the upper body, with arms pumping back and forth with a greater swing and range of motion, helps tremendously with momentum.

**Foot landing.** You can get more power through the glutes on your power hike if you land on your entire foot. For speed, it is best to stay on your forefoot or midfoot.

**Relax.**

If you live in a place without hills, and you know you have three long climbs in your race that will take you a few hours each, a treadmill may be your only option. No one likes that idea, but time on the treadmill will be well spent. It will get your muscle groups ready, even if not in the same way that trail running can fine-tune them; however, you will be actively shaping and preparing your muscles for what is to come. Other options include stairs, stadiums, and overpasses.

## Descending

Descending can be great fun; for many runners, it is their favorite part. An aggressive descent can make up a lot of time in a race, especially if you really step on the gas and push it. As for myself, I feel most alive when I'm running downhill fast. It's an incredible feeling, a beautiful dance. But you need to practice to get it right because it's a lot harder to master a good downhill than a good uphill.

The number one thing to bear in mind—and perhaps the hardest to master—is to allow gravity to do most of the work for you, at points even *all* of the work. This sounds easier than it is. It is difficult to master due mostly to twin inherent fears most humans have of falling and of going too fast. Becoming confident with fast descents takes training. But trust me, it is something that will evolve and improve over time if you work at it.

**EXPERT TIP**

Eat at the top of a climb. You will need that energy for going downhill.

Although I love the descent, to be honest, I'm still not a great downhill technical runner. But, that said, I won the Hardrock 100 in 2012, which is widely considered one of the most technical ultras in the world. I know my descents can be my weakness, so I practice to make sure they don't hold me back.

## Training for Descending

Runners often end up slowing down, leaning back, and braking on descents, thereby creating more work for their bodies. Staying relaxed is key. Again, as with ascents, set your gaze 5 to 10 yards ahead, and even farther when the footing is smooth or after you gain enough confidence. The moment you start braking is usually the moment you start looking too closely at your feet; suddenly you cannot see what is ahead or around you, and this prompts an instinct to slow down. To avoid this, keep that optimal gaze out in front of you and try to let your weight carry you down the trail.

**EXPERT TIP**

Practice with short downhill sprints. Choose a steep downhill section to focus on. Run 2 minutes downhill, hard, then stop and recover. Repeat.

As with skiing, white-water kayaking, and mountain biking, the ability to move quickly down a grade is about finding a line through the rocks and terrain. You see ahead of where you are, and that allows you to set up, preparing your body with gyroscopic anticipation, adjusting your weight for the next several steps.

As I go down, I am constantly searching for the best place to land my foot. I am gauging whether a rock will move or if it is a safe plane, or I am seeking a flat area between the rocks. If you are keeping a fast pace and are light on your feet, the rocks won't move when you land on them because you are not putting much force on each step. It is only when you begin to brake and plant

## TECHNIQUE TIPS **FOR THE DESCENT**

- Landing on your midfoot or forefoot is ideal for a quick cadence and leg turnover. You can slow your pace by taking more rapid steps, a kind of double step, if you will. More contact with the ground, even when quick and light, serves to control your downhill speed with minimal impact.

- Landing on your full foot means a lot of surface area on the ground strike, which is yet another gear for you, like a downshift that slows you down. This can be a very good thing, for example, when footing is sketchy or when you feel fatigued. It's reassuring to know you can go back on your full foot and slow down quickly when you need to. Practice this to gain confidence.

- If the terrain is technical and rocky, try rotating your foot laterally, or outward, into something like a duck stance. This increases stability and can prevent an injured ankle. When you roll your ankle, you usually roll it laterally. Opening up your stance makes that less likely.

- Maintain breathing and concentrate on staying relaxed. In particularly gnarly sections, I often find myself tensing up and not breathing. This means less oxygen to the brain and, for me, often a consequent fall. Remember to breathe!

- If wind or speed makes your eyes water, as they do mine, particularly at altitude, wear a visor and/or sunglasses to help block air as you speed along.

- Spread your arms wide and hold them out to maintain balance—think of an airplane. Holding your arms in this way also helps you feel the flow and rhythm as the trail kicks you one way or another. You'll need to make sudden lateral moves to keep your balance, and wider elbows will help you maintain your center of gravity.

- Look where you want to go; your body will follow.

your feet that the rocks start to move and cause instability. When moving correctly down the hill, you are over the center of your body, landing on your midfoot and maintaining balance. When you lean back to brake, you upset this balance, increasing the likelihood of slipping backward and falling. You also put more strain on your quads and lower back in this position, causing them to fatigue more quickly. Don't fight gravity; let it work for you. The downhill really is one of the highlights of trail running, so don't let fear or inexperience hold you back.

## INTENSITY TRAINING

### Hill Training/Strength Work

Many ultra events include hills and substantial inclines, so you will need to prepare for those climbs. You will build a tremendous and much-needed amount of strength from hill training. Hill work will also prepare you for what it feels like to negotiate repeat hill challenges. Doing hill reps and building up those big muscle groups in your legs will correspond directly to efficiency on race day. Hill training in these plans means 2 to 3 minutes of uphill running at an all-out effort, and then repeating this a specified number of times, perhaps 3 to 12 times depending on the workout. While this may sound like speed work, the hill will slow you down and make you work for it, so I consider hill training repeats strength work as opposed to speed work.

Practically speaking, you can loop your strength work into an easy day, for example, running easy to a designated point, doing 6 hill repeats, and returning easy. You can also locate stairs or a hill on your route that is a quarter-mile stretch of uphill and make that a repeat within your run. That way, you allow yourself a solid warm-up and then a pleasant cooldown afterward. Of course, on inclement days or if you can't find convenient hills or stairs, a treadmill is another option.

## Speed Work

Why even bother with speed training for an ultra? It's a valid question. After all, the pace at which you will run your ultra is likely not what you would consider speedy, at least when compared with a 10K, half-marathon, or even marathon pace. But take it from me: Speed work is very much worth your time and effort, and it provides benefits for more than just your pace on race day. Speed work, done consistently and appropriately, builds running efficiency and leg turnover, makes you fitter and stronger, and prepares you for moments in your ultra when you will be called upon to run harder, whether due to adrenaline or to a need to pass somebody on single-track or to shake off a runner behind you who is throwing you off your game.

Speed work in the training plans in this book involves spending a relatively short but dedicated time running at your hardest effort. I find that fartleks—the Swedish word for "speed play," in which you use variations of fast running for long periods in lieu of structured intervals—on an easy or even downhill grade work well because they best replicate conditions in an ultra. You can do speed work on a track if that is what you are used to; however,

> **EXPERT TIP**
>
> Speed workouts are great to do with others. You are going to be asking yourself to push harder, and let's face it, for most of us it's tough to pull out a best-effort pace by yourself. Training with others removes some of the dread that can accompany speed work and also ups the accountability.

I find that training for speed on a dirt road or trail replicates ultra conditions and unstable ground in a way a track does not.

Attacking these speed workouts at a hard effort will not only build your strength but also train your body to switch up gears and incorporate different muscle fibers, something that your ultra will call on you to do somewhere along the way. In the plans in this book, you will see speed work mixed in with tempo runs and long runs.

## Tempo Runs

A tempo run is a steady effort for a specific time and distance, with a pace likely just below your 10K pace. It should feel like a strong but not all-out effort. Tempos are a key component of training and go a long way toward building speed and strength. They are especially useful in training for an ultra because tempo runs, like ultras themselves, require you to test yourself over a longer distance and time. They will increase your ability to push yourself over a longer time at a steady, consistent effort. They take a lot out of you, so they will appear only about once every 7 to 10 days in the training plans; a tempo run is almost like being in a race, which means you will need time to recover afterward.

I enjoy doing my tempo runs with runners who are of equal ability or even faster than I am—training partners who are capable of pushing me more than I would push myself. Tempo runs also work well with a group, where runners alternate taking the lead and making sure everyone is maintaining an overall effort for the designated amount of time. This is especially important for trail tempo runs. It is easy to lose sight of pace while you are on the trail, with the climbing, descending, and uneven terrain, so it is nice to have others to help you stay on that tough pace.

## EASY RUNS

Easy runs are the key to building your core and foundation, and your training plan will include a lot of them. In fact, the majority of the runs in the plans are easy runs. Easy runs are done at a comfortable pace that allows you to carry on a conversation with ease, at an approximately 60 to 70 percent exertion level. It's not a time to worry about pace, to check your watch frequently, or to push yourself; in fact, it's a good time to put all of that aside.

Rather, during an easy run you have the time and space to listen to your body and feel out how it is bouncing back from your prior week's training or racing. These runs are by nature more relaxed and more fun, giving you time to socialize if you wish or to be alone and reflective or to think about nothing at all. And while easy runs can be very routine, in the best sort of comfortable way, that doesn't mean you have to do the same run over and over: Easy runs give you the flexibility to decide where to run, on what terrain, and for what mileage. They are a great time to run with different running partners, perhaps someone who doesn't necessarily push you as in a tempo run or a long run, but someone you simply enjoy getting outside with.

My running normally has a competitive angle to it—it's what I do. But on easy runs, I can let that go and simply run. I often go on 2-hour easy runs with my wife, spending quality time together, or with a group from the running store, with everyone there more to be social than to bring out our competitiveness. Especially if I'm coming off of a race or getting back into training after an absence, these runs are great; besides being enjoyable, they allow me to work at a pace or on muscles that I normally might not. On an easy run you can chat and catch up on what's going on in the world of running, explore new routes, or stop and catch your breath without pressure. Easy runs are a time to let go of the urgency and pressure of training. They may remind you, as they do me, why you love to run in the first place!

While you may feel that easy runs are simply junk miles or a waste of time that takes away from "real" training, in reality they are anything but a waste. You are adding to your foundation, not to mention building strength and muscle memory. In addition, these runs keep you in a routine and, when preceded by a hard tempo or speed workout or race, remind you what easy feels like.

Something I enjoy about easy runs is the flexibility they allow. I can, when necessary, break mileage up throughout the day or use an easy run to tack on additional mileage. After a hard race or tempo run, I might go out later that evening for a 5- to 6-mile easy run. Some days you may feel crummy and swap out a hard workout with an easy run, adding in the harder workout on a day when you feel better. I will discuss this further in Chapter 8.

## LONG RUNS

Many people get into ultras specifically for the long run; these are the folks who crave mileage and may already spend one or both weekend days out running long whether they are training or not.

A long run is by definition, well, long. Specifically, it may make up about 30 percent of your weekly mileage. Or, if you are doing back-to-back long runs, these could total about 50 percent of your weekly mileage.

What's especially useful about the long run is that it requires a significant effort and a lot of time on your feet, but it is not the actual race; thus, you have the luxury of being able to practice for your race, experimenting with nutrition and seeing how your body reacts to long miles and hours on your feet. The physiological benefits aside, the long run will give you confidence that you can handle what is to come.

Whether you go with a group or prefer some uninterrupted solo time is an individual decision. Approach the long run in the way that will allow you to get through it best. After all, it should be enjoyable—anything you do for 4 to 5 hours electively should be fun!

Logistically, long runs present a few key challenges, with fueling being the main one. Lining up a few long races during your train-

 ## How long is **long?**

While you need time on your feet and miles on your legs to prepare for an ultra, in deciding on your mileage, the sky it not the limit. At some point, if you run too far, you reach a point of diminishing returns, where you are simply getting overtired and not productive. In a marathon, 18- to 20-mile long runs are appropriate. For ultra training, the longest long run should be about 60 to 70 percent of the distance you will race. However, a training run of that magnitude for, say, a 100-miler is a lot to bite off. As the training week progresses, you can do back-to-backs, logging two long runs in a row.

These BTBs, as we call them, are as much about time on the feet and time being out there as they are about mileage. You will learn what it takes to muster mental as well as physical energy when you think you have none left. You will also experience the caloric demands of hours of exercise and figure out how to eat and drink on the run when that might be the farthest thing from your mind. These runs will build massive amounts of confidence and a physical strength that is unparalleled.

ing—say, a 50-miler to gear up for your 100-miler—is a great solution to the fueling logistics problem. Your fueling and hydration will be taken care of through aid stations along the way. If you don't have a race, you can instead organize your long run by creating loops that allow you to return to your car or home, where you have stored fuel and drink. Or, if you'd prefer an out-and-back route, you can drop a cache at the far point earlier in the day. Finally, you can try organizing a run that passes through towns along the way, where fuel is available for purchase. I did a run near Seattle once that took me across several mountains. At the base of each mountain was a small town, with at least a small grocery or gas station. We'd fuel up in town and then head up the next mountain. It was a lot of fun and certainly added another interesting element to the run.

## MILEAGE—QUANTITY VERSUS QUALITY

In a perfect world, you would have both quantity and quality. But when it comes to training for an ultra, quantity has the edge over quality. There, I said it. Time on your feet is crucial. The miles do not all have to be pretty, but you must be out running for an extended time to replicate and prepare for the massive challenge your event will entail. Can you get away with doing fewer miles? Maybe, but chances are high you will pay for it in the end with fatigue, possible injury, and a slimmer chance of performing consistently well in your race.

Nevertheless, quality runs do play a key role in your training. Quality comes in when you train in a specific way for your event. Following the Pine to Palm 100-Mile Endurance Run, I am often approached by disappointed runners who are mystified at why the run did not go as planned. "I trained so hard!" they say. After a bit of investigation, it usually becomes clear that while they put in the miles, they did not train specifically enough for the event, such as for the diverse terrain or temperature. Your miles and training should be targeted to what you are preparing for. That makes for quality running.

One of the best ways to combine quantity *and* quality is by adding a prep race to your training schedule. A race event forces you to get on your game and push yourself during the miles rather than slogging along unmotivated and unfocused.

## PREPARATORY RACES

Injecting supplemental races in your calendar as part of the buildup to your goal race is a good idea for several reasons. One, these are in a sense supported training runs, where you have aid stations to supply you with food and drink, and therefore you can go farther and push yourself longer than you might be able to if you are going it alone. Two, a race will familiarize you with the feeling of running on different trails than you're used to. That not only is good practice for your upcoming race but also can be quite rejuvenating.

During a preparatory race, you can also practice what you are going to do on race day—what you will wear, what you'll put in your drop bag, what you will eat—all without the pressure of it being the real thing. Prep races may also help you to deal with pre-race nerves so that you are calmer going into your goal event. Finally, a race adds a fun, competitive aspect to training that you won't get doing the miles by yourself.

When I was younger, I would sometimes race as often as twice a month during training. I just loved being out there and pushing myself in a race situation. The downside, of course, is that I would often get caught up in the thrill of placing well or running with friends above my fitness level and thus push myself a little too hard, which I began to notice would compromise the A race that was my primary goal. So I pulled back on the number of races and the distances. But, undoubtedly, shorter races helped me to build up for the 100-milers. They gave me a lot of time on my feet and the incentive to push myself harder while getting in solid 30- to 50-mile training runs that I may not have done on my own.

For all these reasons, I strongly advocate prep races and have suggested in the training plans points in the schedule at which they would be appropriate. How they fall in the periodicity of your training is important. You need to have sufficient training to build up a base for these races, and you also must have time to recover afterward. If you put yourself out there to do a race and can't help but push yourself, that is understandable, but know that you can't do that too many times or you will undermine your goal race.

## RECOVERY/REST DAYS

When training for an ultra, you may be asking more of your body than you ever have before, and you will do so across several weeks. Perhaps unsurprisingly, too many runners end up injured before they even get to the start line. Part of the reason for that is that they do not include enough rest and recovery. You must give your body a chance not only to rest after a hard string of workouts but also to rebuild and repair. This will help you rebound more quickly and make you stronger for the next round.

So, when you see recovery days in the training plan, remember, they are placed there strategically. Don't ignore them! That said, there is some flexibility, which I will discuss in more detail in Chapter 8.

For example, if you do not want to take a day entirely off, there are times early on in the plan, during your buildup of base miles, when it is appropriate to do what is called "active recovery"—meaning an easy run. However, when you begin calling on your body to do the really long runs later in the plan, you simply must do all-out recovery.

 ## Am I **overtraining?**

Overtraining can occur when you have not allowed for a sufficient amount of rest and recovery after a hard effort either in a race or in training. Many times this is not apparent until after multiple days of hard running or numerous races with too short a turnaround. Signs of overtraining include sleeplessness, overall sluggishness during daily routines, and negligible gains in training efficiency and speed.

Because ultra training is primarily about managing the stress you are putting on your body, dealing with the increased load without getting sick, injured, or burned out, a key part of your success comes from early detection. You need to hone your ability to sense early signs of injury or illness, stopping a niggle before it flares up enough to sideline you.

When you begin a run that is supposed to be easy and your heart rate races from the first half mile, that is your body telling you that you shouldn't be pushing. Conversely, when you have a speed session planned but are unable to get your heart rate into the desired zone of suffering, that, too, is a sign to call it a day.

Try taking your resting heart rate first thing in the morning while you are still lying in bed. This provides a baseline measure by which you can gauge your relative fitness as you progress in your training, as well as an early indication that you may be burning the candle at both ends. A higher than normal rate is a sign to take the foot off the gas. When your resting rate returns to normal, you can be more confident that you are ready to rock.

## TAPER

Rest and recovery prior to your race are pivotal. Tapering is the final period in your training program, when you strategically ease off of training for the purpose of being primed and ready for race day. By this point in your program you've put in the hard work, faced many challenges, and called on your body in different ways. Now is the time to wean off that heavy training, getting more precise with your last workouts, which will be of a shorter duration, and becoming mentally and physically poised for your event. It's easy to lose confidence when you stop training, but remind yourself that you are not losing anything during this period; rather, physically you are being restored so that you will be able to peak on race day.

Your taper period is the time for banking calories and sleep. While many runners dread tapering and the associated slothful feeling that comes with reduced activity, try to see past that and remind yourself that it is a key element of your training, just as important as the speed sessions and long runs you logged to get to this point. You may find that you have a case of the "taper tantrums," with muscle tweaks, spasms, and slight annoyances cropping up in those last couple of weeks, but rest assured they are usually temporary annoyances that will fade away come race morning. While you may wish to do low- or no-impact crosstraining such as swimming or Nordic skiing during your taper, it is also an excellent time to see a massage therapist for some treatment, being careful that the therapist doesn't go too deep.

The taper is also a valuable time for replenishing your emotional energy reserves by enjoying family and friends. The time you save by running shorter distances can be invested in your support network. Do favors for the people who help you to pursue your running goals, the ones who will be out there crewing you for or pacing you during your ultra. This will help to propel you on race day.

## WEIGHT TRAINING/CORE WORK

As runners, we mostly just want to run. However, the ultrarunner has much to gain from weight training and core work. Being in good condition throughout the body is important in an endurance event; it's definitely *not* just about your feet. Good, strong posture—which comes from a strong core—will help take some of the strain and fatigue out of being on your feet for hours or even days. You also need good arm and core strength if you intend to carry a heavy pack or poles. Selective weight training, consisting of low weight and high reps, helps build the strength you need out on the course, without adding bulk. Targeted core work, specifically ab work, will go a long way toward preventing injuries and supporting a strong, healthy posture. And because trails are uneven, technical, and often rocky, your core is key to keeping you upright and balanced when the footing gets tough.

I include some weight training and core exercises, such as crunches and hanging leg raises, in my training week. Hanging leg raises in particular are a favorite because they work both the hip flexors and the lower abs. They can also work your lower obliques, depending on how you perform the crunch. The Roman chair sit-up is another great exercise that specifically targets the hip flexors, a group of muscles that you are asking to lift a heavy weight over and over again for hours during an ultra. But the beauty of crunches is that they can be done with no equipment and just about anywhere. While I do go to a gym a few times a week, I also try for 100 to 200 crunches and sit-ups every day, just on my own at home.

Weight work is also great for ultrarunners. To avoid upper-body bulk, I generally take a less-is-more approach, with lower weight and higher reps. To increase the difficulty, I will add reps instead of more weight.

## Crosstraining—yes or no?

If you love to bike or go to the gym, I'm not going to say that is altogether a bad thing. You can improve your circulation, work your muscles, and get a good cardio workout without all the impact of running. Crosstraining can be a great way to maintain your fitness during recovery from an injury or to avoid burnout. Maybe on an easy run day, the weather is inclement and you choose to spin instead. Or you've rolled an ankle, so you substitute a bike ride for a run workout. However, the training plans in this book are specific to running because, in the end, to be a good runner and get to your goal, you need to run.

Specificity in your training counts. I'm not against supplementing that specificity, if that is what you enjoy. However, if crosstraining is getting in the way of your ability to carry out the training plan, then I would suggest that it is too much. If, for example, you choose to do bike rides during the week and miss your runs, then maybe you need to assess whether you really want to commit to training for an ultra. Or else be more realistic with the goals you are setting for your completion of the event.

That is not to say that supplemental or complementary training, such as weight training, yoga, or core work, will detract from your specific run training. It is only when the nonrunning sessions take away from your ultra training that you need to evaluate your priorities.

As for the lower body, you can gain power through your glutes by doing high reps of squats while holding a bar or dumbbells. I don't normally focus much weight work on the lower body, but I do include some eccentric quad training on the leg extension machine at the gym. After picking a reasonably resistant weight, I hold the extension to muscle failure. I suggest starting with a weight that allows you to maintain the extension for 45 seconds and increase weight from there. Eccentric muscle action occurs as a braking or oppositional response to concentric (shortening) action. The muscle is elongated, which helps protect joint structure. I am particularly diligent about this type of lower-body work if an upcoming race includes steep downhills, such as at the Western States 100-Mile Endurance Run. Know your course, and change up your weight and strength training depending on what your race has in store for you.

## ROAD AND TRAIL—MIXING IT UP

Typically, we train on what we like. That is human nature. For many—even most—ultrarunners, we seek out trails, not road. And so when you enter a trail race, you may do so thinking you'll run trail. But in my Pine to Palm race, for example, 40 percent of the distance is run on dirt roads. This catches some runners by surprise. I understand that—most ultrarunners adore singletrack; it is entertaining and challenging in a way a road usually is not. It is also easier on the legs.

In a race, if you come to an unexpected road, this can make the event seem harder, reduce your confidence, and even zap your motivation, precisely at a time, often deep in the race, when you need those things the most. The impact can seem even harsher, depending on where you hit a road section during your event. If, for example, you are at mile 30 and already feeling pretty beat up, those feelings can be magnified both mentally and physically on a tough, unforgiving stretch of pavement.

One of my first ultras was the Washington State University 100K. The first half of the event was entirely on paved road, followed by some uphill time on gravel and then the final miles back on a paved road. I had trained a bit on pavement, but not to that magnitude. Not only was it hard on my legs, but there was a dangerous allure to the flatness of it, one that caused me to go off my pace, pushing too hard. The pounding of running for an ultra is hard enough, but it is made that much harder on road. By mile 30, I'd blown up; I had never run a marathon, but I would have equated it to hitting a wall and feeling unable to take another step. Once we started uphill on that gravel road, I was reduced to walking, despite much prodding from my pacers and crew. I simply was not prepared for how big a shock the flat, rock-hard road would be to my body. I had run roads to get to trails during training, but that exposure was limited to a mile or two. What I discovered the hard way was that after hours of running, road *really* hurts! Everything that was sore was multiplied many times over.

The point is that you need to have some level of hardening to make it through. The Leadville Trail 100, for example, has some significant flat sections, some on pavement, and even the best athletes can be waylaid by them. So if you know there will be some road in your event, make sure you are adding in enough road training. For example, run on trail for 2 hours and then finish with a 5-mile stretch on pavement. Or maybe start with a 5-mile warm-up on the road prior to the trail run. Or make one of your tempo runs a road run. These training strategies will help you combat being affected by some of the less pleasurable aspects of running on the road.

## STRETCHING

Stretching is a controversial subject. Recommendations based on research and your best running pal's advice range from do it but only before your run, to definitely do it, but only following your run, to not do it at all. Let's face it, we tend to believe advice that supports what we are already doing. I personally support the literature that says I can run as much as I want to and don't need to stretch. I don't think I'm alone in that. However, it behooves us to look at the debate a little more closely.

In training, there will be times when your body feels fatigued and overused, when you are not recovering well from workouts, or when you have excessive tightness that needs relief. While I am not someone who stretches regularly, I find that these are the times I look to stretching. Because it is generally agreed that stretching "cold" is not a good thing, I will stretch after a run, or after some time in a sauna or a warm shower, when my muscles are warm. However, that warmth can lead to a sort of false flexibility, so take care not to overstretch.

Practically speaking, I stretch the bigger muscle groups—calves, quads, and a little into the hamstrings. I hold each stretch for approximately 10 seconds and repeat it up to 3 times. In a sauna, I may extend these practices (carefully) because the deep heat allows longer holds.

My lack of stretching over the years has not led to injury. However, I can't speak for everyone. If stretching has been a part of your history, stick with it. Otherwise, light stretching may be sufficient and your best approach. Using a foam roller or another self-massage tool is beneficial, providing relief for sore, tight muscles.

Moral of the story: Stretching is like nutrition; it is very specific to the person and his or her unique predilections. No one thing works for everyone.

## DO I NEED A COACH?

The aim of this guide is to explain in a clear, uncluttered, and comprehensive way what you need to know to execute your best ultra and achieve your goal, whether that is to try an ultra for the very first time, to move up to a new distance, or to podium in your A race. I have included tips, advice, training plans, and the best (and worst) of my experiences as a way to answer common questions, allay fears, and build strength and confidence.

However, a coach can also be an excellent resource, especially if you have highly individualized needs—for example, wanting a plan that accommodates significant time constraints, or coming back from an injury, or training for an event in a highly specific way with someone who has intimate knowledge of the course. In such cases, a coach may be a great idea. With a coach you can work one-on-one and deal with your limitations and expectations together. Commonly, coaches work up an individualized plan for you, whether online or in person. In some cases you have access to the coach every day, to bounce ideas off of him or her or to ask questions.

I have never used a coach, mostly because when I started training, few ultra coaches were available. Today there is far more expertise available to the average runner. Many coaches have run these races and can get you up to speed on course specifics as well as dialing in a plan for a certain distance or course.

If you do not work with a coach, this book allows you to set yourself up with the knowledge base and training you need to achieve your goals, and it gives you a helpful background on variables you might encounter in these events. But remember, too, that part of the challenge—and the fun—of getting through an ultra is learning how to deal with things for which you cannot be prepared. Embrace that; it is one of the things that makes ultras so intriguing and so very rewarding. That does not mean you should not come prepared. Rather, just remember what they say about the best-laid plans. They are bound to go off track, so expect the unexpected and do not let it undermine you and your race.

# 3
# NUTRITION
# AND
# HYDRATION

≡

WHETHER AT MY SHOE STORE, ON A RUNNING PANEL, IN A magazine interview, or just on the street, one of the first questions people ask me is this: "What do you eat and drink when you train and race?" Understandably so. It is one of the most vital elements—and perhaps greatest mysteries—in ultrarunning. No self-respecting ultra manual worth its electrolytes would fail to include a chapter on nutrition and hydration because, while there are myriad factors in succeeding in the ultra distance, if there are two that can utterly make or break your ultra, it is these. So getting them right is crucial. What makes them really tricky, however, is that there is not one right way to fuel and hydrate. Some basic rules apply to everyone, but in the end, what works best for me may not be what works best for you. Thus, what you will find in this chapter is some general advice about how to prepare, as well as some tips and advice from my own experience through the years, both successes and failures, trying to figure out the nutrition and fueling that works for me. Much, however, is up to you, and as with many aspects of ultra training, intelligent experimentation is your best friend.

## ONE GUY'S FUELING STRATEGY

I've got no label when it comes to what I eat and drink. I don't follow a special diet and I don't have allergies. I have not chosen to follow a paleo or vegan diet, and I have no problems with gluten or other sensitivities. This has allowed me to eat a fairly mainstream, nonfussy diet, which is helpful for the limited time I have when it comes to training, running the store, and tending to family.

There is no denying that what I eat and drink, however random at times, has had a strong influence on my performance. And while I do not follow rigid rules when it comes to diet, there are a few things that I always do to keep that influence positive. I make it a priority to eat a substantial amount of calories when training and recovering. I always have a bagel, pretzels, or almonds handy throughout the day to keep me fueled for my runs. That way, even if I have an impromptu date with the trails, I am fueled and not worried about having a heavy stomach from a meal or, on the flip side, forgoing a meal to take a run. If my meals aren't measuring up to my mileage, I feel it from the first step, and this self-awareness helps me stay on top of deficiencies. Also, I put a lot of emphasis on carbs in my daily meals when training. I eat carbs when I run, and even before I run, because I find they make me feel energized for a sustained period. I would go so far to say that for a number of years I lived off of what I call the B-cubed diet: burritos, bagels, and beer.

I admit, getting my strategy down has taken a lot of practice and trial and error. In the beginning, I did not think about it much at all. When I first started running marathons, I knew very little about fueling. I remember slamming hard into the wall at about mile 18 or 20. I had run out of sugar sources and felt completely spent. I was still able to pull off the marathon distance, but it was unpleasant and far from my best. But let's just say I could get away with it—barely.

The ultra distance won't let you get away with that. You *will* hit the wall in the ultra. And you will hit it over and over again; it is almost impossible to avoid. But when you do, it is not as much a bodily function disaster, as happens in a marathon, as a mental acuity issue. You feel mentally jumbled and glassy-eyed, probably uncoordinated, and perhaps sick. The trick is not so much avoiding this altogether but rather minimizing these effects as much as possible, through best hydration and nutrition practices. Smart practice during training will make you a more efficient calorie-burning machine and help you jump these hurdles during your race.

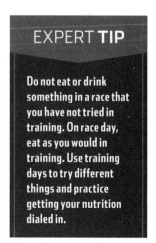

EXPERT **TIP**

Do not eat or drink something in a race that you have not tried in training. On race day, eat as you would in training. Use training days to try different things and practice getting your nutrition dialed in.

## HOW MANY CALORIES DO I NEED TO RUN AN ULTRA?

To put it simply, you probably need more calories than you are going to get. Much depends on how fast you are running, your own physicality and fitness, and how long you are on your feet. I can't prescribe an exact number of calories. But whatever your particular requirements, there is only so much you will be able to physically take in. Realistically, 400 calories is probably the most you are going to be able to get in per hour. If you are running, a full stomach is not desirable. Food and drink consumed on the run will be sloshing about, and the calories may end up getting ejected, via your bowels or vomiting. So finding the right number of calories is an art as well as a work in progress. A central part of your training, therefore, is feeling out the correct number and kind of calories for you.

The wonderful thing about getting fueling right is that your body lets you know by the sense of well-being you feel during your race. You are so in tune with your body in an ultra, functioning at a heightened state of awareness, and so it becomes fairly easy to discern the role that food and drink are playing in your performance and overall state of being. If you are taking in sufficient calories and staying on top of your hydration, you feel good, by which I mean having a steady flow of energy free of big drops and jags, continual mental clarity, a relaxed, happy stomach, and no cramping.

When I won Western States in 2007, I credited my fueling. Throughout the event, I just felt so good, in all the ways I've just mentioned, and this allowed me to execute the entirety of my race strategy with aplomb. I've blamed losses on fueling as well.

In sum, fueling counts. A lot.

There will be times during a race when you have to force yourself to stick to the fueling plan. Consider your food your medicine, which in a way it is, and find a way to get it down, because every calorie counts when you're running an ultra. Pinch your nose if you have to, so you don't smell or taste it. (If what you have planned to eat is now making you vomit, however, it might be time to employ your fallback plan.) Oreos were a major part of my eating strategy when I ran the John Muir Trail in 2013. I loved them when we started out, but

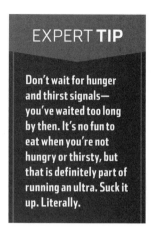

EXPERT **TIP**

Don't wait for hunger and thirst signals— you've waited too long by then. It's no fun to eat when you're not hungry or thirsty, but that is definitely part of running an ultra. Suck it up. Literally.

I got unbelievably sick of them halfway through the adventure. At that point, though, we were in a remote area, and Oreos were what I had. So I swallowed them, but it became very much like a terrible force-feeding by the end. If possible, come up with alternatives and put them in your drop bag. The Pine to Palm has about 10 drop bag spots, more than enough to allow you access to a variety of foods all along the way. For most of us, a handful of chips and a few squares of PB&J offered at the aid station won't get us very far. These allow you just enough energy to throw yourself back to the wolves. It is a smart idea to plan for and carry your own nutrition.

## WHAT NUTRITION DO I NEED?

There are so many choices. So how are you going to craft your race strategy around those many options? An important part of training is figuring out how your body would like its nutrition to be delivered. Bars, gels, chews, whole foods, or some particular combination of them all are options; it depends on what works best for you.

Let's take a closer look at the different options.

## Gels

I have experimented with many different sources of fuel over the years, but personally, I'm a big fan of gels. For me, these are the easiest, quickest source of energy and sugar, with a relatively minor impact on the stomach. Although I am not sensitive to any foods, follow no special diet, and have a highly tolerant stomach, I still like to keep things as simple as possible on race day. Too, gels are lightweight and high on the ease-of-use scale, which is key for me.

My partiality for gels developed through experience. Early on in my career, I ran some races in which my stomach went quickly south, much to my disappointment and surprise. This would happen in particular when I was racing at altitude, which is itself quite hard on the stomach. Getting dehydrated at altitude is easy if you don't eat and drink early and often. On top of the stomach problems dehydration can create, you pay a further price if you try to catch up by stuffing the stomach when it is not primed for it and in a moment when it least can handle it.

EXPERT **TIP**

Gels should always be taken with a drink—water rather than electrolyte drink is best.

I've also experienced problems simply eating what may have been the right thing but at the wrong time, for example, downing a dense, 400-calorie energy bar right in the middle of running at 80 percent of my maximum heart rate. Let's just say it didn't stay down for long.

With these mistakes under my belt—which in a few cases definitely played a part in costing me a race—I decided not to leave things to chance. Gels allow me to gauge my calorie input very specifically, and they go down quickly and relatively painlessly.

They are easy for the body to process, which means you aren't taxing your digestive system, using up energy that you'd prefer to use for running.

A common complaint about gels is that they are monotonous and make eating a bore, or they become unpleasant as you try to psych yourself up to down your 20th gel without vomiting. I can't argue on the monotony front. So I switch up the flavors, which helps. I sometimes place gels in carbonated sodas, which help disguise the gels and add extra calories. Also, I sometimes substitute chews (discussed later) as a way to break out of the tedium. Chews, which come in smaller calorie increments, allow me to customize calorie delivery even further. For example, if I am bursting at the seams with sugar at a point in the race, I can dole out the sugar more slowly with chews than I can with a gel. However, chews demand, well, chewing, and it is much harder to masticate when you're also trying to breathe. For that reason, I find that chews are very useful in training, but gels are the best on race day.

Gels contain about 100 calories each and are easy for your body to assimilate. The amount and type of sugar vary, from maltodextrin to brown rice syrup to honey. The type of sweetener determines how much energy you get from them over time. Honey is very quick acting but levels off relatively fast. Maltodextrin offers a slower release of sugar over a longer period, since it takes time to break down those sugar chains.

Note that some gels have caffeine. And while that caffeine can give you a nice boost just when you need it, and can certainly be part of your arsenal, you will want to beware of caffeine overload, which can cause upset stomach, anxiousness, and even adrenal bonking. So know which ones have it and which ones don't.

As you stand before the generous offerings of various gels at your local sporting goods store, ask yourself a few questions. In your experiments with gels, how do they sustain your energy? Do you prefer a particular flavor or no flavor at all? How are they on your stomach? What else is in the gel? Amino acids? Electrolytes? Caffeine? All of these will have an effect on the overall usability of the gel.

## Gel Alternatives

### Fat-Based

These include foods such as nut butters. Because they are a fat source, they are high in calories, containing about 800 calories for 4.5 ounces. For many runners, they are also more satisfying than standard gels, in a comfort food sort of way, and often are quite tasty. These generally don't contain much besides fat and calories, although some include caffeine. Their rate of absorption is much slower and more sustained than that of standard gels.

### Fruit-Based

These are made from pureed fruit, which is easily ingested. They taste a lot like baby food (another popular option for ultrarunners), and many are all natural, which appeals to many runners. They act a little more slowly than honey but faster than maltodextrin. Best of all, they typically taste a bit better than standard gels and are easier on the stomach.

### Baby Food

Baby food was a go-to option for many ultrarunners before the gel industry revved up and there suddenly were many convenient options on the market. Baby food provides a heartiness and wholesomeness that some runners crave, as well as a few more calories.

Although it can be expensive to buy off the shelf, you can fairly easily make your own, which is far more cost-effective. Just puree the vegetable or fruit you want, put it into a small, sealable plastic bag, and sip from a small hole in the bottom.

### Energy Chews

Chews offer a similar mix of ingredients as a standard gel but in reduced amounts and in a smaller, gummier form. Many runners like their similarity to gummy candy, making eating them a more pleasurable experience than sucking a viscous solution from a wrapper. I use them often in training,

EXPERT **TIP**

I take a gel or some chews right before a run or race to get in some precious extra calories. After that, I ingest two to three gels per hour.

but on race day, I find chewing a challenge late in the race and so usually opt for these only in the early miles or before race start.

### Sports Bars

Bars make a satisfying pre-run or pre-race breakfast because, unlike gels, they feel like a meal or a hearty snack. They also make a great recovery food following hard workouts and races, when you require calories but your stomach may not be able to handle a whole meal.

There are bar options for whatever your preferences, from vegan and gluten-free to whole food to nuts and seeds to power bars. Just as with the ingredients, the calories range widely, so spend time with the label. And test out the bars during training. Some will be easier on your stomach and take less time to digest, so make those your race day choices and save the others for less-intense activities or when you have time to consume them while at rest. Another benefit of bars is that they are easy to consume in parts, saving what remains for later. Note that unlike with gels, eating a bar on the run can be a bit tricky. You need the right amount of fluid in your stomach to digest it. And you have to do some serious chewing, which can feel challenging later in a race or run. Finally, consider the temperature when bringing bars in your pack as your snack of choice. Some can get quite rigid in colder temperatures, making them even harder to chew.

## SALT

Your body requires and craves salt to keep it functioning properly. In ultra racing, it plays a couple of crucial roles, including helping you to maximize fluid absorption, to stave off muscle cramping, and to replace salt lost from sweating.

The science on salt in endurance sports has thus far been pretty inconclusive. Some studies point to salt's effectiveness in combating cramping and muscle fatigue, while others have concluded it has little effect on these. I am not a scientist, so my experience with salt is on the ground, not in the lab. However, I have found salt to be extremely effective when it comes to cramping.

In 2011, I ran Zane Grey, a brutal, uphill 50-miler in Arizona. It is an April race, and temperatures were in the 80s. There are only six aid stations in this race, and they are spaced far apart, with about 10 miles between stretches. The course is technical and slow, adding to your time between stations. This is a race, therefore, that requires you to stay on top of your fueling and hydration.

I had been running harder than usual all day because the leaders were running particularly fast. I was without salt tabs, trying to hydrate with two bottles, and finding myself out of water several miles before the aid station. At mile 40—and at this point in second place—I started cramping as I ran up a long hill. It got worse and worse until I felt as though I was turning into the Tin Man, trying to run even as I watched and felt my muscles seizing. Still in race mode, I kept trying to take steps, but I reached a point where I was just standing in place, unable to move. I had resorted to licking the salt that had collected on my arms when a fellow competitor handed me two salt tabs. I took them, and in the time it took to swallow them, plus maybe 20 seconds more, the debilitating cramps had completely subsided. I was amazed. By this point, I had about 7 miles to go, and while I remained on the verge of cramping, it did not happen again. Call me a believer.

Maintaining your body's electrolyte levels during a race is certainly something to attend to. In mild temperatures and in cold temperatures, I find I am able to get sufficient salt from other sources, staying on top of sodium in those conditions by relying on what's in my drink or in gels. If the temperature sits above 80 degrees for a large portion of the day, however, I begin to add in salt tablets as a further preventive measure. How many and how often vary depending on how extreme the weather conditions are. For example, during Western States 2013, when temperatures were consistently between 90 and 100 degrees, I ran the first 3 to 5 hours relying on salt from my drink and from gels only; after that, I began taking two salt tablets every hour.

Unless you have particular medical concerns such as high blood pressure, there is no need to worry about taking in too much salt. Your body will expel what you can't use. Sodium intake recommendations

## SODIUM CONTENT

- Salt tab—200 mg/tab
- GU—250 mg/serving
- Gatorade—70 mg/serving
- Potato chips—170 mg/15 chips
- Pretzels—380 mg/serving
- Chicken broth—770 mg/can
- Teaspoon of salt—6,000 mg

**Note:** Sodium amounts are approximate and will vary by brand, flavor, and serving size. Check the label.

vary, but for me, 200 milligrams per hour in mild conditions is OK. In warmer temps, I take 400 milligrams per hour.

Many endurance drinks contain salt, and manufacturers are adding more all the time. However, especially in warmer temperatures, you are probably not going to get enough salt in your drink alone. Too, it is difficult to monitor the amount you are getting. Similarly, adding table salt to food at aid stations—such as dipping a boiled potato into salt or grabbing a handful of pretzels—is tasty but hard to quantify. Salt tabs are a painless way to deliver your salt and the easiest method for determining how much salt you are taking in. The salt comes in a thin casing; don't open up the tabs, and don't put them in water. Just take them as you would a pill.

## A WORD ABOUT WHOLE FOODS

I don't think anyone would make the argument that gels or chews taste better than whole food. Real food is just more pleasurable, giving many runners a sense of comfort; also, the slower rate at which it enters your bloodstream means the energy it provides is prolonged. If whole food has worked for you in training, then by all means continue with it on race day. Just remember that foods you might enjoy or be used to are unlikely to be out on the course, so prepare your drop bags accordingly or make sure your crew has what you want.

I eat whole foods for breakfast before a race begins, such as oatmeal, muesli, or a bagel. This makes me feel comfortably full initially and also provides long-lasting energy. Additionally, it helps the body absorb any last-minute hydration that will become invaluable later in the day and expands the stomach, readying it for further ingestion.

However, I usually don't continue eating whole foods during a race. For one thing, I find it bulky to carry solid food in training and don't want to experiment with it in racing. Also, at the heart rates

## NUTRITION-DENSE AND PORTABLE
## WHOLE FOOD OPTIONS

- Whole-wheat avocado wrap
- Hummus on pita
- Turkey wraps
- PB&J
- Dates wrapped in bacon
- Hash browns

- Cinnamon and cream cheese wrap (tortilla, cream cheese, cinnamon sugar)
- Coconut rice balls
- Almonds
- Pierogi (potato or cheese)

at which I'm running, dropping a burrito in the stomach is a challenge (although Scott Jurek famously does so). While all that salt and fat and calories may sound good, especially late in a race when you are so depleted, I've discovered the hard way that it's not a good fit for me.

Once I was deep in a race and had long since lost my appetite due to altitude and a sour stomach. I had no desire for gels, which were the main part of my fueling strategy. As a result, I had failed to get sufficient calories in and was on a fast downward slide, with my energy level and clarity so low that I was in danger of not finishing the race at all. As a last resort, my pacer begged me to eat some solid food, handing me the remnants of a quesadilla he had with him. I remember being on an uphill climb, and all my body wanted was to eject that food. I had to get my heart rate under control, slow my pace to a crawl, and sip splashes of water with every bite, but I ate it, and those precious calories helped boost my spirits mentally and preserved my place in the race, allowing for a strong finish.

## CAFFEINE

Caffeine can offer a nice energy boost on race day. How and when you administer it depends on what you are used to. If you normally drink coffee in the morning, I would not recommend skipping it the day of the race or you may find yourself with a headache and some symptoms of withdrawal. Because I am a morning coffee drinker anyway, I normally have a cup of coffee about 30 minutes before race start. I will go to great—even ridiculous—lengths to ensure I have coffee on race morning, but if coffee is not available for some reason, I will be sure to take a gel that has caffeine in it leading up to the start of the race.

A popular strategy with some elite athletes is to hold off on caffeine until late in the race; they swear they can obtain a stronger boost from it at that point, just at the moment when reserves are flagging. But, again, I'm more of a proponent of "go with what you know." In my experience, if I drink coffee in the morning, I get a great energy boost then, as well as some additional mental acuity, and it helps to access fat stores in the middle of the race. That is what works for me. Experiment to find what's best for you.

If you are not a coffee person, bars, gels, pills, and drinks such as Red Bull and Mountain Dew are alternatives for getting your caffeine hit.

To administer my caffeine intake throughout a race, I ingest caffeinated gels, which I generally do not start taking until about a third of the way through a race. From that point, I take one every 2 hours or so. Finally, a warm coffee late in a race can do triple duty, opening up your airways and soothing a dry throat while supplying caffeine.

## HYDRATION

As you probably learned back in elementary school, the body is composed largely of water, up to 60 percent to be precise, which serves several essential functions. Water's contributions to saliva production, digestion, temperature regulation, waste management and disposal, and oxygen delivery are particularly relevant and vital in distance running. Your body will use up a lot of water in training for and racing an ultra. The most obvious reason is that your body sweats from exertion or warm temperatures, but several other sneaky culprits also dry you out: altitude, fluid lost via respiration, and mucus membranes being taxed on dusty trails. So hydrating isn't just about drinking to slake your thirst. By the time you feel thirsty, you are probably already falling behind on consuming fluids, and it can be hard to catch up. Add to that the not altogether unlikely possibility that you will experience diarrhea or vomiting later in your race, and you may be well behind the eight ball before you know it.

Precisely how much water you need will vary under different conditions; however, it is crucial to have a plan of attack and know how much you need to drink and when. On race day, if conditions are what I consider ideal (60 degrees and cooler), I like to start the event carrying a 16- or 20-ounce water bottle, with a plan to drink and refill it once an hour. If temperatures are hotter, or in races where the distance between aid stations is longer, I will carry two water bottles, one filled with water and the other with an electrolyte drink.

In training, I plan on one 20-ounce bottle of water for 2 hours. If my run is longer, I might customize the route so that I can get water along the way or do a water drop beforehand, leaving bottles at strategic spots on the route.

But the best-laid plans do not always go smoothly. Despite years of experience, I have misjudged what I should carry, fumbled and spilled a full bottle, or underestimated distances between aid stations or the distance I was covering on my training run. I have had to back off a podium-busting performing knowing I was short on water, recalculating my pace for my own health and for the sake of just being able to finish the race. For sure, one of the more amusing facets of ultras is nimbleness and the need to think on your feet and have a plan B. When it comes to hydration, however, there isn't much room for error, so anticipate what you need and how you are going to ensure that you get it.

At the inaugural Bear 100 Mile Endurance Run in 1999, I remember having to switch from competitive mode into survival mode as my dad paced me to the 75-mile aid station at Copenhagen Basin. We were heading into unknown territory as darkness fell on the course and route markers became as meandering as the trail we thought we were following. As we fumbled around a drainage, crisscrossing time and distance, thoughts of squandering the lead I had so earnestly built throughout the day raced through my head. That sense of disappointment and disquiet left little room for critical thinking. At the same time, the tough terrain and altitude were wearing hard on my determined father, who was pushing his boundaries as well. We ended up stumbling into an archery field parking lot, discovering that it wasn't in fact the trailhead we were looking for. Now desperate, we began to forage around the parked cars and a couple of unlocked truck toppers for water. Now, trespassing is sometimes unavoidable when you're lost in a race, but tampering with private property in the outskirts of Idaho is another thing entirely. I remember my dad mumbling something about swiftness and thanks, as he reached into the back of a small pickup and pilfered a few ounces from a jug of water, and then, just like that, we fled into the night. I would never suggest such deeds for any of you because you will be far better prepared; you will have your courses, distances, and aid planned accordingly and will be able to keep your wits about you. I share this rather embarrassing impropriety purely for educational purposes.

## Water Versus Sports Drinks

Sports drinks make it easy to replenish your electrolytes. They taste better than water, which may encourage you to drink more and more often, and they supply you with energy. Does it matter whether you drink water or a sports drink? Is one superior to the other? The answer is one of personal choice and taste. I do use sports drinks, often craving the sugar and counting on the calories, but I do not drink them exclusively in a race. The sugar in them does not provide long-sustaining energy, which can mean a peak and crash in energy flow. I find them hard on my stomach, and there are points at which the last thing I want to do is have another sip of *that* taste, which then ends up putting a noose around my calorie and hydration intake. To combat this, I may hold off on drinking a sports drink until later in a race, or else I bounce back and forth between water and a sports drink throughout the day.

## Recovery Drinks

Following a hard effort, your body needs to replenish its glycogen stores, rebuild muscle, and stave off additional breaking down. The right recovery drink can help get this process started. The ideal

### RECOVERY DRINK IDEAS

- Chocolate milk
- Protein powder mixed into a fruit smoothie
- Coconut water with protein powder
- Hal's Peanut Butter Smoothie

    1 large banana, frozen and cut into 1-inch sections
    1 cup chocolate milk
    1 tablespoon creamy peanut butter
    Blend the ingredients for 30 seconds or until smooth. Easy!

recovery mix will include some carbs and protein as well as some electrolytes. You don't need much protein, by the way. You can only handle about 20 grams of it at a time; your body will get rid of the rest or require too much work from the kidneys to process the excess, so don't go too far. Chocolate milk is an excellent and economical choice, with an ideal mixture of sugars and protein. If you can't digest cow's milk, look for almond or soy milk substitutes. For maximum benefit, consume a recovery drink within 30 to 45 minutes of finishing a race or a long training effort.

## Beer

Although beer doesn't get a high ranking as far as hydration options, if you don't overdo it, there is nothing wrong with a post-race pint. Beer will supply you with some needed carbs and has the added benefit of being a little bit numbing, which can be a welcome relief after a race. The great running guru Arthur Lydiard advocated beer for his athletes, so if it fits your persuasion, don't feel bad for taking the edge off of a long day of training with some suds. That said, remember that beer can be dehydrating, so just go easy with it.

# 4

# GEAR

I HAVE EITHER WORKED AT OR OWNED A RUNNING SPECIALTY
store for a big chunk of my adult life. As an ultrarunner, I get a lot
of time on my feet to test and think about the products I use and,
in turn, am rather picky about what I carry in my shop and sell to
my customers. Gear matters. It can ruin a race that you've trained
for, flushing away months of hard work. As such, it is just as
important for you to know what to put on your body as it is for you
to know what to put in your body. You need to educate yourself on
the best shoes, apparel, hydration system, poles, lighting device,

and electronics for your individual needs. You are particular about your training schedule and diet, so apply that same focus to assure you have the right gear for you; it will pay off in countless ways.

## SHOES

Running, for many of us, begins and ends with shoes. People don't simply associate running with shoes; in many ways, they actually *identify* with their shoes. After all, shoes are about the only thing you really need to be a runner. And after you've logged a lot of miles in a pair, they can begin to feel like an extension of you or, perhaps better, like a solid training partner, whom we rely on for cushioning, traction, security, comfort, and protection.

When it comes to shoes, there are too many models and types to say which is definitively better than another. Much comes down to running form, body type, weight, shoe shape, running surface, weather conditions, injury history, and personal preference. No two people have exactly the same feet, and thus no one shoe works for everyone. Shoe fit is based on such factors as foot shape, foot type, and running stride, which don't easily translate from one person to another. So listen to other runners' testimonials, but don't rely on them. When it comes to certain elements such as durability or traction, group wisdom can be incredibly useful. However, fit, comfort, and performance are strictly individual; it's best to choose your shoe after diligently trying on a number of models, regardless of what your training partners are wearing.

When it comes to fitting your running shoe, go ahead and eschew the standard "I wear a size X." You may wear an 11 in a street shoe or a dress shoe but find that you need a 13 in a running shoe. What matters is not a prescribed size but the fit and the feel. You will be in this shoe for hours or possibly a full day or more; you require something that fits your foot well, is comfortable, and allows room for swelling and splaying and flexibility.

The right shoe may not prevent injury, but the wrong shoe can certainly lead to injury. I learned this the hard way, unfortunately. In the middle of a hugely important race for me, my first Western States 100, in 2001, I experienced excruciating pain as my toes jammed repeatedly against the front of my shoe on the downhills.

## Do I need a trail-specific shoe? **?**

Road and trail shoes have much in common. However, there are some highly practical features to a trail shoe that make one well worth your consideration. Many trail shoes give you extra lateral stability on the upper, as your foot moves from side to side on rough terrain, over rocks, on roots, and through streams. Keeping the foot as stable as possible minimizes blisters and the risk of rolling an ankle while crossing uneven ground. Also, as you tire, you will benefit from the extra support a trail shoe can provide. The reinforced toe on most trail shoes, made of tough rubber, does a good job of protecting your toes when you smash into a sharp rock. The tread on the outsole can give you better grip and control on uphills and downhills and when accelerating and braking. And although you may not think you need it, the additional traction will help as the miles wear on and your feet and legs lose performance. Some outsoles have modified rubber compounds that offer better traction on wet surfaces or that protect against rock penetration, while some companies go so far as to layer the midsole with a nylon, fiber, or plastic shank to shield the underside of the foot.

Yes, all this adds some weight, but only a few ounces, and given the amount of protection you can gain, that extra weight is worth it.

Western States is a largely downhill race, with temperatures that reach the triple digits at times. Naturally, my feet swelled in these conditions. I endured it as long as I could but ended up borrowing a knife at an aid station and cutting off the front part of my shoes to make running sandals that gave me the space and relief I needed. I ended up losing eight toenails from all that jamming against the front, but at least I finally had alleviated the pain. Unfortunately, this unexpected opening in the shoes allowed for an enormous amount of dirt and rocks to get in, which created its own problems. Lesson? Buy a shoe with a fit that anticipates the stresses of an ultra.

I strongly recommend going to a specialty running store, where you will find not only variety and depth of choice but also customer service that often includes stride analysis. Be sure to ask if there are any ultrarunners on staff because they will understand your specific needs.

During an ultra, you will spend many hours in your shoes. Thus you need a pair you trust and have been running in, which—

**EXPERT TIP**

Break in a new shoe at least two weeks before racing in it.

given the number of miles you cover in training and racing—might mean multiple pairs of shoes. Not only will you need to watch for wear and replace your shoes as needed, you may actually want different shoes for the same race. For example, you may want a minimal shoe for the race start and opening miles and then another shoe with some padding later in the race. That's fine, but remember, you need to dial this in with the terrain of the course. Your favorite road shoe may be more cushiony and comfortable,

## Are my **shoes worn out?** ?

You are relying on shoes for protection and comfort. As the foam breaks down, a shoe gets quite flat. The outsole may look fine, but the midsole may be worn down. If you aren't sure if your shoe is ready for the recycle bin, try the "fold test": If you can fold the forefoot like a taco, and get it to bend beyond a right angle, the shoe is compromised.

but make sure it's in line with the demands of the trail or road you will be racing.

Finding the right shoe is a process of simply trying on a lot of them. Running stores sometimes even allow and encourage you to spend time running in them on trails. Ask about their policy and take advantage of any opportunity to test a shoe thoroughly before you buy it. You may need to kiss a lot of frogs before you find the prince or princess you are seeking.

And if you really like the way a particular shoe fits, feels, and rides, consider getting multiple pairs. Manufacturers will frequently tweak models, and the changes may alter your favorite pair. So if you can afford it, consider stocking up on the make and model you like to ensure a seamless transition when your old pair wears out.

## CLOTHING

Fashion and ultrarunning haven't always mixed. And with all that you are asking your body to do, looking good clearly takes a backseat to feeling good. Happily, companies are catching on to the popularity of ultrarunning, making smarter clothing that not only looks great but, more important, serves the unique needs of the ultra-athlete in several key ways.

Exposure is a player in the game when you are spending an entire day, two days, or sometimes more outside. At various moments in an ultra race or long training day, keeping warm or staying cool will become key. It's important to be prepared for that with the right clothing. For warm days, you want fabric that breathes and wicks moisture away from your skin. Materials such as engineered mesh allow for optimal, strategically located ventilation along the spine and under the arms, enhancing your body's ability to regulate its temperature in hot weather. Wicking materials can be crucial in humid conditions. When the cold hits, you need to be ready with layers to keep you warm. Wool, especially merino wool, which doesn't itch and is machine washable, can be worn as a base layer for thermal regulation that transports sweat away from your skin, and it has natural antimicrobial characteristics to ward off body odor. Wool tops and bottoms now come in a variety of weights so you can wear articles of clothing made from this wonder fabric in both cold and hot weather.

And, of course, what would life on the run be without some inclement weather? There is the rain, when you will want to shelter the body with a waterproof, breathable jacket if warding off cold is going to be a concern. The problem with truly waterproof jackets is that it's hard to keep from getting wet from sweating on the inside of the fabric, where the jacket has created a steamy microclimate. You will need to know how much rain you are likely to confront, whether it is going to last the whole race or just be a tolerable mist. If it is a warm rain, you may be better off getting wet and wearing less, staying light and fast. In drier climates a microfiber, highly breathable jacket with a hood, one that packs down small enough to fit into your fist, may well do the trick, so check with locals to find out what they recommend for the time of year of your race.

Many ultras take place in the mountains, even at high altitudes, where the weather can change drastically in a moment and layers of protection become key. Many race directors require participants to carry mandatory gear, such as a shell, hat, and gloves. Take these seriously; they could be lifesavers in a pinch. Temperatures can plummet at elevation, and rain can quickly turn to snow. Wind can rob an already depleted body of warmth in no time, so be sure you have what you might need under the forecasted conditions, and err on the side of caution.

Comfort is equally important. Anything that touches your body is something to consider carefully in planning for long races. You know the way that seam in the underside of your sleeve rubs on your armpit? No big deal, right? Think again. What might not be a problem over a few miles can become not only aggravating but downright painful 30 miles in. I learned this the hard way during the Ultra-Trail du Mont Blanc in Chamonix. Because shorts were not allowed, I was given a pair of leggings for the race, capris that I was assured were unisex. The female version, I was told, was "virtually like the male version." I can tell you unequivocally that halfway through a race like Mont Blanc is not where you want to find out that this is not true.

The capris were thin and rubbed in all the wrong places. I tolerated this for a time, but there came a moment when I was rubbed raw and could no longer stand it. For several miles, I ran with my hands down my pants, keeping tender parts separated from the fabric. This was awkward and certainly not good for my running form, to say the least. Finally, out of sheer desperation, I emptied the snacks out of a ziplock bag I was carrying and used it to create a barrier down below.

The lesson? With all your gear, try it on and put some miles on it before you show up in it to race.

## Performance

As with compression, the performance aspect of any one piece of clothing has not been convincingly proven. However, if clothing keeps you warm, dry, cool, or comfortable, I would argue it lends a very positive boost to your performance. Along those lines, there is something to be said about looking fast and how that parlays nicely with picking up the pace on race day.

## A Short Word About Socks

Socks matter. Believe it. I'd go so far as to say that socks need to stay static more than any other item of clothing come race day. You get what you pay for, so pay for a worthy, durable pair to keep you comfortable and safe from the rigors of long-distance days.

Finding the perfect sock for you make take some experimentation. Runners become very particular about their ideal sock, and their allegiance to thick or thin, wool or synthetic, high or low almost smacks of religious conviction. Be sure to find your own truth through the miles of trials and trials of miles.

If there is anywhere you should steer clear of cotton, it is here. Cotton does a great job of absorbing water, but that's about it. Where it fails is in moving that water away from the skin and allowing it to evaporate. The material becomes bulky and heavy and tends to bunch, creating friction, which causes hot spots and blisters.

When it comes to ultra mileage, whether long training days or racing, you are asking your socks to do a lot, and so you need them to hold up. With articulation features in the design— left and right designs, arch bands, Y seam construction in the heel, and high thread count—they quite literally will hold up. Choose a sock with durable materials and quality construction.

## EXPERT **TIP**

Many shorts now include a compression two-in-one brief to help prevent chafing. The fabric is slippery on your skin and dries quickly. Also, look for pockets, which make a convenient place to stash a key, gels, or tissue, among other items.

If you are looking for some mild compression to keep the sock from moving around in your shoe, you can find that, too.

## Gaiters

Dirt, rocks, sand, and other debris have a tendency to make their way into your shoes. Once inside, that is where they will stay, irritating you until you finally stop, remove the shoe, and shake out the offending detritus. Run, repeat. Gaiters are handy items that you slide on over your shoes; they do a good job of covering vulnerable openings where debris can penetrate.

As a rule, I do not wear gaiters because I tend to adjust my laces a lot when running, and gaiters sometimes cover access to those, making lacing more troublesome. In some places, however, such as areas with lots of sand or scree or snow, gaiters are an excellent and practical way to protect yourself from the nuisance of having to keep removing your shoes. Besides keeping out debris, gaiters can also help keep your shoes from untying and prevent thorns or sharp rocks from ripping at your shoe's mesh upper. If you are doing some bushwhacking or running on an overgrown trail or in high alpine areas among loose rock, gaiters can be superhelpful.

Look for a gaiter that's geared toward a trail shoe as opposed to a hiking boot; it won't have as much strapping or external material and will be far more flexible and lightweight.

## Compression

"Compression" is certainly a buzzword, and you have probably noticed compression gear all around you: taking up lots of space on store shelves, out on the trail, and as you toe the line on race day. Calf and arm sleeves, tights, shorts, socks, all snug fitting and sometimes brightly colored, are everywhere. What's the deal? Is this a fad? Or is it a must-have innovation that can help you to recover and perform at your best?

My answer to these questions is … sort of. From my own on-the-ground experience, as well as knowing a bit about the science, I view compression gear as effective in some ways but not a panacea. Undeniably, by the time you have run for 12 to 34 hours, you can rest assured that your legs are not in the shape they were when you arrived at the starting line. Anything that helps restore your legs to pre-race condition, especially if it can prevent serious harm, is most welcome.

Compression for recovery is the most publicized facet of running compression and the best tested. However, there is no conclusive scientific evidence that compression staves off fatigue when used during an event or that the reduction in muscle vibration helps prolong performance. And the studies that do show performance benefits from reduced vibration don't take into account the necessary restriction in motion or flexibility that accompanies the compression that would achieve that state. But tests show that recovery gear can help minimize the damage and discomfort from post-race swelling. And, I promise you, after a 50- or 100-mile race, there is going to be some post-race swelling.

You can also utilize the gear for recovery during travel following a race. Because many ultras are held in fairly remote locations, an extended travel period is often inevitable. Tests have shown that compression helps to keep blood from pooling, a common occurrence when you are sedentary for long periods in a car or plane. This can literally be a lifesaver, but note that calf sleeves do not prevent pooling around the ankles; more coverage, whether from a sock or compression tights with feet, is a better bet.

The convenience of compression gear may be its strongest recovery selling point. After a long run or race, I enjoy nothing more than to plunge into a nearby river or stream. There are recovery benefits (not to mention the sheer delight of cold water on fatigued limbs) to doing so in the first hour following your effort. Practically speaking, however, it can be hard to find an ice bath to soak in right after a race. With compression gear, you are already wearing it, or can easily put it on, making it a highly convenient recovery tool.

As for compression wear's ability to improve performance, such as faster times, nothing has yet been proven. Still, there's no proof that it does not improve performance. And even if speed isn't the payoff, when you are talking about 50 or 100 miles, simply minimizing the vibration or muscle damage so that you can complete the distance is sometimes a way to keep you in the game.

I use calf sleeves and compression shorts because they give me a sense of control over the inevitable muscle breakdown that results after miles of running. I also find that they minimize my fatigue and make me feel a little more efficient when I run. Finally, I find that the calf sleeves, in particular, help late in a race when I inevitably move from running into a less flexible, less rhythmic form that I call an "ultra shuffle"—that point near the end of a long day when form starts to fall apart, putting strain on your legs and calves in particular.

In the end, my thought on compression gear is this: When you're talking about the potential for easing the strain of hundreds of thousands of steps, what's the harm in using it?

But as with any gear, experiment with it in training and under conditions that simulate those you will find on the course, including temperature, so that you know what works for you come race day.

## HYDRATION: PACKS VERSUS WATER BOTTLES

Hydration is no minor matter in ultrarunning. Indeed, by some counts, it is nearly everything in ultrarunning. So the seemingly trivial question of whether to carry a water bottle or to wear a hydration pack in order to get fluids is of much greater importance than it may at first seem.

Hydration packs have much to recommend them. They allow you to carry more fluid, which means fewer stops for refills and longer runs. And while carrying water can be heavy, the pack disperses weight nicely across your back or across your lumbar region, if you use a waist pack. With packs you get the additional benefit of having your hands free, which can be instrumental on the trail, allowing you to climb more safely, protect yourself if you fall, and maintain good form. Finally, packs allow for far more storage space, giving you a place for a light jacket, snacks, or your phone.

However, I'm a handheld guy. For one, I find the pack a little bit suffocating. You want it firmly cinched around your chest so it doesn't bob around on your back, but if it's too snug, it can make you feel constrained. Also, your back, which is a large and effective cooling area, can get too hot when you are wearing a pack. This also causes the fluid in the pack to get quite warm.

Finally, there is the ease of use of handhelds. When you come into an aid station during a race, the handheld is quickly and easily filled, and you're off again. With a pack, you must unclip it, take it off, open the hatch, fill it, secure the bladder top, remove excess air from the reservoir, and then put it back on, readjusting the straps for fit. It's a process—with some room for error, unfortunately, as I found out the hard way on a few occasions.

In 2004 I was running the Barkley Marathons in Tennessee. This race is as tough a 100-miler as there is. It consists of five 20-mile loops with 100,000 feet of elevation change. And, yes, this was in Tennessee. There are a number of idiosyncratic challenges to this race, but the main one is that there is no aid to rely on. I do remember the race director telling us before the start that he hoped to place water jugs at the halfway point of the loop by the time we got there. It did not sound like a certainty by any stretch. Essentially, you rely on your own water and nutrition.

I finished the first 20-mile loop in just under 9 hours. On that course, 9 hours for 20 miles is a good time, believe it or not, and I was in the lead pack. But it was far from a comfortable 20 miles, in large part because I had been forced to complete that extremely difficult loop without most of my water. Going into the race, I had decided to use a new prototype hydration pack that my team manager had given me the week prior. I did not have a chance to practice

EXPERT **TIP**

Air in your pack's bladder means you must work harder to both breathe and suck up water at the same time, which can undermine good hydration. The sloshing sound can also be very annoying to you and anyone running nearby. To avoid these problems, fill the bladder, turn it upside down once, and suck the air bubble out by drawing on the mouthpiece. This will assure that every sip you take is liquid only.

with it before the race but figured, what could go wrong? You fill the bladder, close the industrial-sized ziplock, and enjoy for hours, right? As the miles ticked off, however, I noticed I was wet and figured I was perspiring far more heavily than usual. What I failed to realize was that a small leak had developed in the inverted bladder, and the wet substance running down my shorts and legs was not perspiration at all but all the water and electrolytes I would get on that go-round. To make it more desperate, turns out the race director hadn't made it to stash those halfway-point water jugs after all. It was a long, long 9 hours.

That race, along with a few other bad experiences, means that my track record with hydration packs isn't very good. I've stuck with handheld bottles.

You may have a different preference. Remember, if you are going to use a pack, fit is key. Runners come in all shapes and sizes, and packs should not be treated as one-size-fits-all; try several on for size before purchasing. They are also often gender-specific, for good reason. Women typically have significantly smaller shoulders and narrower latissimi dorsi and chests than men, so do check to see if your favorite brand of pack comes in both a male and a female version.

## TREKKING POLES

Once popular only in Europe and with hikers, trekking poles are now seen regularly in the hands of ultrarunners in the United States. And with good reason—they serve several valuable purposes. On uneven trails, they can help you keep your balance. On steep descents, they offer you braking power and minimize the impact of downhill pounding. On ascents, they encourage arm movement, which helps you run more efficiently and allows your arms to take some of the workload off of your legs. They can also encourage good upright posture for better breathing while ascending. At night or late in an ultra, when you are otherwise exhausted, they help you feel your way through challenging trails and to just feel a lot more powerful and confident, having four points of contact on the ground rather than only two.

Although they may look big and cumbersome, most poles fold down to approximately a quarter of their length, making them easy to carry. Made of lightweight materials, they can be tucked away when you need to stow them.

If you are going to use trekking poles in a race, practice with them first. While they can definitely make you more efficient, if used improperly, they can instead slow you down or get you into trouble, especially on the downhill. You need to establish a rhythm when using poles. Work to find your stride using them, timing your poles so that they are moving in concert with your feet, in a way that feels natural.

I used poles during my 2013 run across the John Muir Trail. They were particularly handy when I was feeling destroyed after high ascents, steep descents, and sleepless nights. As my legs were feeling shaky and worn out, I was able to incorporate more strength from my upper body, which helped ease my fatigue and boosted my confidence when my balance felt off.

If you plan to use trekking poles in a race, be sure to check the race's specific guidelines. At the Ultra-Trail, for example, you are allowed to have poles, but you must carry them with you for the entire race. You cannot hand them off to your crew at any point or retrieve them from a drop bag in the middle of the event. Some races see poles as providing such an advantage that they do not allow them at all. So before you become dependent on poles, make sure they are allowed in your chosen event.

## FLASHLIGHT/HEADLAMP

In the course of running ultra distances, almost inevitably there will be times, likely extended periods, where you will be running in the dark. Along with fatigue and altitude, nighttime running is the top challenge that will slow you down.

Staying on the trail and being able to find the confidence ribbons and other demarcations indicating the correct way to go is obviously key throughout the nighttime hours. Therefore, choosing your illumination and being prepared to back it up are crucial.

Headlamps provide you with strong light while keeping your hands free. When affixed to your head, the light is directed wherever you are looking. Unfortunately, some runners find headlamp bands constricting and even a bit painful after hours on the

EXPERT **TIP**

In races, confidence ribbons are brightly colored tape or ribbons hung on trees or posts to reassure you that you're on the right track.

trail. There is also the problem that if you move your head to look left or right, the trail ahead goes dark. A good solution for some is to put the headlamp around the waist instead. With light affixed to your waist, you can move your head around, but the light stays constant, keeping the trail lit out in front of you. This also lowers the angle at which the light is shining on the trail, which effectively improves depth perception.

On a very technical trail, I might double up, wearing a lamp around my waist and also carrying a handheld. This allows stable visibility in front and around me; at the same time, it lets me look around for sometimes-difficult-to-spot course markings.

You can have the best and brightest light there is, but it isn't going to help you if the light goes out! You must carry multiple batteries or multiple lights during an event or when training in the dark. Take into account that late at night temperatures typically fall, and cold weather drains batteries more quickly. Carry a spare

## CHOOSING A **HEADLAMP**

The amount of light, or number of lumens, a lamp puts out is a key factor in choosing your headlamp. Yes, bright is good, but you do not necessarily require the brightest lamp that is available. Remember, the more lumens, the shorter the battery life, although many lamps allow you to toggle through different brightness settings so you can adjust the brightness as necessary. I prefer something more minimal, which will have a longer life and also may be lighter weight. Two lighter headlamps might be better than one large one with a heavy battery pack.

set of batteries or an extra light on your person rather than depending on a drop bag down the line.

During one ill-fated race, I placed a headlamp in a drop bag that I left where I expected to be before the sun went down. Tough terrain and a few other unanticipated problems slowed me, and soon it was dark and I was without illumination. I tried to stay close to a runner in front of me who did have a light, but I kept tripping, falling, and struggling to catch back up, even though he was kind enough to slow down a little. Suffice to say, I felt very grateful—and more than a little sheepish. This snafu unraveled the entire race for me. I went from being in third place and feeling great to completely falling apart. It was a hard but important lesson to learn how this technical difficulty can stop you flat.

## WATCH

For many runners, their watch is as integral a part of the running experience as their shoes. We've all seen the pose: one hand at the other wrist, poised to strike when the start gun goes off, and then that same hand right back at the wrist, turning the device off the moment the finish line is crossed. For many of us, running, mileage, and time are seamlessly intertwined, the watch like a constant companion and touchstone.

I'm not sure we want to live or die by our watches—or any gear, for that matter—but they do come in extremely handy. If in a race or training run you are shooting for certain splits or an overall time, or needing to ensure you get to the aid station under the deadline, then a watch is indispensable. It is also essential when it comes to monitoring your nutrition and hydration.

Once, during a 100-mile race, I decided I wanted to run completely by feel, so I went without a watch. By 3 or 4 miles in, I knew it was a terrible mistake. Having not trained without one, I was pretty much at sea. My pace was not the problem—I had that pretty well internalized. It was staying on top of when I needed to take another gel and having no wrist-mounted reminder that it was time to drink my water. While not wearing a watch was certainly freeing in some ways, it was also frustrating and became problematic, with my nutrition suffering over the miles.

**EXPERT TIP**

Women's watches are smaller, lighter, and less noticeable on the wrist. Many watches made for men are unnecessarily huge and heavy and can be quite uncomfortable.

You don't have to spend a lot on a watch. Being able to tell the time is obviously key. But another useful feature is a chrono/stopwatch function, which allows you to time laps and monitor your pace during training. Many runners like to have a GPS function on their watch (see below), but this of course adds to the price and is not absolutely necessary.

## GPS

GPS devices can provide you with an incredible amount of information. Whether you want to download your workout, view your entire route, check your current elevation, see where the climbs were on your run and how long they took you, compare sections of your run to other sections or past runs, map a route, avoid getting lost, locate a specific point, or merely brag on social media, the right GPS makes it all possible.

## GPS: **A CAVEAT**

GPS, while amazing, is not infallible. You can get a pretty terrific reading from a GPS, but remember that connectivity is not constant, especially in trees, down in steep ravines, and in the mountains. Thus, your data can end up a bit skewed. Don't live or die by the GPS reading, and (I say this as a race director) don't simply assume inaccurate measurement of the course.

The competitive advantage of a GPS, which allows for real-time elevation, pace, and mileage calculation, is that you can gauge your race far more precisely than ever was possible in the past. Another very practical function is guidance. If you preprogram your route into the watch, it can help you stay on the right track. This is especially handy at night or in high alpine clouds or fog, when it can be very hard to see the trail. Some devices also have a built-in compass so you know what direction you are going.

The more functions that a GPS has, the shorter its energy life may be. A few models may last the whole ultra. However, if you rely on the GPS, then I advise having multiple watches. As a way of reducing battery drain, consider resetting the connectivity by having it communicate with the available satellites less frequently, say, every 60 seconds rather than every 3 seconds. This will save the battery, although the reading will not be as accurate, depending on your terrain. In the Badwater 135 Ultramarathon, much of which occurs on road, the infrequent signals won't dramatically affect the reading. For the Wasatch Front 100 Mile Endurance Run, set deep in the mountains, your data won't be as reliable.

## MUSIC

A lot of us, myself included, head out to the trails or quiet country roads to escape for a while from the noise and commotion of our busy lives. However, ultras demand an extraordinary amount of time alone with your thoughts, both in training and in the race itself. Music can be a pleasant distraction from some of the pain and monotony of these long hours, helping to eat up large chunks of time that otherwise would be spent staring at the horizon.

EXPERT **TIP**

A music mix works great for long hours on the trail. Select some tunes that pump you up and others that calm you, then set your device on shuffle—it's nice to be surprised.

Besides being a pleasant way to pass the time, music has been shown to be a small but significant performance enhancer. A popular study from 1997 conducted on the effects of music on athletic performance found that it did indeed have the power to affect performance.[*] Music can act both as a stimulant, to keep your energies high when they are flagging, and as a sedative, to ease anxiety about how much farther you have to go, about the

---

[*] Peter C. Terry and Costas I. Karageorghis, "Psychophysical effects of music in sport and exercise: An update on theory, research and application," in *Psychology Bridging the Tasman: Science, Culture, and Practice—Proceedings of the 2006 Joint Conference of the Australian Psychological Society and the New Zealand Psychological Society,* ed. M. Katsikitis (Melbourne, VIC: Australian Psychological Society, 2006), 415–419.

## HAL'S **PLAYLIST**

- Bob Marley, "Want More" (*Live at the Roxy*)
- John Butler Trio, "Treat Yo Mama" (*Live at St. Gallen*)
- Kanye West, "Jesus Walks"
- Tedeschi Trucks, "Midnight in Harlem (Swamp Raga Intro)"
- Mos Def, "Ms. Fat Booty"
- Black Crowes, "Remedy"
- Michael Jackson, "Don't Stop 'Til You Get Enough"
- Modest Mouse, "Float On"

competition around you, or about your physical discomfort. Music allows you to tune out much of the internal "noise" that can be defeating after miles and miles with miles more to go. Music also serves as a metronome, allowing you to keep pace and form by timing the cadence of your footsteps when you are mentally and physically exhausted. There is nothing like dancing down a rocky trail when you are otherwise feeling spent.

Remember, though, that it's important to be able to hear the people around you, especially in a race situation when they are trying to get around you. Be cognizant of others, and keep the music level low enough that you can hear who is coming up behind you. You can wear an earbud in only one ear to allow you to hear ambient sound, especially when running solo or at night, when safety is a concern, whether because of wildlife or human threats.

# 5

# MAINTENANCE,
## SELF-CARE,
## AND FIRST AID

**WE ALL LEARN FROM THE SCHOOL OF HARD KNOCKS, AND** believe me, I've been schooled out there over the years and countless miles. One thing I've learned is that all ultras hurt, but they do not have to leave a physical mark, other than that proud hobble you may sport for a few days following the race. A stitch in time will save you in a big way, and knowing how to take care of yourself is crucial because a bad blister, mangled toenail, raw chafing, rolled ankle, sour stomach, or worse can sideline you and ruin all your hard efforts. Knowing how to avoid or deal with common ultra maladies will allow you to reach your objectives.

# PREVENTING AND CARING FOR SMALL INJURIES

## Blisters

Blisters are one of the most common foot problems that can occur on race day. Although it is a seemingly small thing relative to bigger catastrophes such as dehydration and heatstroke, even a dime-sized blister can quickly make your day miserable, at the very least, or can even end your race. The foot has a great amount of neural feedback and is therefore extremely sensitive; that repetitive pounding on a sore can be excruciating. (Blisters may also be telling you something about abnormalities with your feet, foot strike, and weight dispersion over time, so don't take them lightly. A hot spot is not always a symptom of poor moisture management.)

The best way to deal with a blister is to not get one in the first place (see sidebar on page 89). When blisters *do* appear, several smart techniques, both offensive and defensive, are appropriate. For excellent, detailed recommendations about general foot care, pick up the book *Fixing Your Feet* by John Vonhof. Vonhof's aggregated insights from his own and others' ultrarunning experiences serve as an indispensable tool that goes into far more precise detail than I can here.

Practically speaking, when I develop a blister during a race, I pop it immediately with a pin. Use a pin from your bib, or get one at the aid station. The aid station should also have alcohol and a needle, if you would prefer to be more hygienic about it. A medic or willing volunteer can even lance it for you when you stop for refueling. Puncturing the blister with an unsterilized instrument does pose a risk of infection and is not recommended for blisters with blood in them, which indicates access for a potential infection to reach the bloodstream.

## BLISTERS—**PREVENTIVE MEASURES**

- If you tend to sweat heavily in your shoes, experiment with foot powders, talcs, and wool or synthetic socks that keep feet dry and help them breathe. If you have excessive problems, seek over-the-counter hyperhidrosis topicals or consult your local podiatrist.

- Experiment with lubricants such as Bodyglide or petroleum jelly. Some feet work better with powder than with lubricant, so trying different products to find what works best is key.

- Socks are important! Wear well-fitting wool or synthetic technical socks that wick away moisture. Sock thickness is a highly personal preference, so test out a variety to find what works best for you, and then stick with that decision come race day. Fit is important, and you will find that excess material rubs and creates hot spots. Invest in socks that fit and work well for you.

- If your feet are wet from a stream crossing or excess sweat that isn't wicking away, consider a change of socks and/or shoes or use a blow dryer at your next stop; aid stations sometimes have one available, but be careful to avoid burns.

- Don't delay getting dirt and pebbles out of your shoe: Stop running and remove the debris. Small grains of sand or rocks can easily create friction or a debilitating wound.

- Wear gaiters, especially if there is a lot of shale, scree, sand, or snow on the route.

- Buy shoes that are large enough for you to run downhill without jamming your toes. If you can feel the end of the toe box with your big toe or second toe while standing, go up a size.

- Lacing is important. Your shoe will shift less on your foot if the laces are snug but not overtightened.

When popping a blister, leave the blister roof intact, and insert the pin at a point where the impact of running will naturally force the fluid out (usually at the opposite end from where the force is occurring). Once it is popped, push all the fluid out, pat the roof of the blister down on the base, and put your socks back on over the popped sore. I don't generally cover the sore because it is difficult to get anything to stay on the affected area; some people, however, find that duct tape or a band-aid is effective in preventing recurrence. Use caution, though, because additional materials in your shoe can sometimes lead to more chafing and discomfort in the long run.

## Toenails

Let's face it, black or missing toenails are something of a fashion statement and a badge of honor for ultrarunners. But do everything you can to avoid them, or suffer the painful consequences.

Your first best defense is properly sized shoes. I wear a size 12 or 12.5 in training, but on race day I wear a size 13. When running tens of miles, especially in hot conditions, there is much you cannot predict. One thing that you can count on, though, is that your feet will swell at least half a size. Moving up half a size and thus giving yourself that extra room in the toe box is imperative. Smashing painfully up against the front of your shoe on every downhill step when your foot is already swollen will traumatize your toenails, separating the nail from the skin. Pre-race trimming of your toenails, straight across and just above where the nail plate emerges from the side nail folds, may help. Cutting the tops off of your shoes is a last-ditch move but an effective solution. However, having open-toed shoes on a trail race is certainly not optimal. In sum, ensure that you have ample room in your shoes going into the race.

## HAL'S **MANITY KIT**

First aid should be positioned strategically around a course. Be aware, though, that medical representation will not be available at every aid station. If something happens, you may be some distance from an aid station or hospital, so it would behoove you to have some basic education on dealing with the wilderness. Be smart out there. Take personal responsibility, and be your own first responder!

There are some items that you will want to have with you at all times or ensure that your crew has them. I always carry a special box that I jokingly call my Manity (you know, like "vanity") Kit in which I keep essentials I want on my person. Your list may be different than mine.

- Aspirin
- Scissors
- Nail clippers
- Tweezers
- Alcohol swabs
- Athletic tape
- Leukotape (rayon-backed tape with an aggressive zinc oxide adhesive)
- Moleskin
- Wipes
- Band-aids
- Duct tape
- Bodyglide/petroleum jelly (petroleum jelly is better in private areas or on feet and is easier to apply)
- Bag Balm
- Antacid tablets
- Extra batteries
- Salt tabs
- Caffeine pill

While toe box space is key, also ensure that the instep and heel feel secure. Lace the shoe snugly, leaving wiggle room for toes, but a secure fit from the ball of the foot back.

If you're in need of a nail clipping, be sure to do it a few days prior to the race. If you clip them the day before and accidentally cut them too short, there is no time for the nails to grown back a little, and running can be painful.

If, despite your best efforts, a nail is hanging loose during a race, remove it at the aid station. I suggest then covering the exposed toe with duct tape so that it doesn't become irritated by your sock.

## Chafing

If you have ever chafed, then you already know how painful it is. It's a feeling you don't soon forget. You probably also have become intimately acquainted with petroleum jelly and Bodyglide as a result. If you have not chafed, consider yourself lucky and do everything you can do proactively to avoid it.

Chafing is caused by the friction between a skin surface and other skin or clothing as they constantly rub together in movement. The raw skin reaction is expedited by sweat or moisture, especially when salt crystals are entered into the abrasive equation.

In a discussion earlier in the book about the importance of trying out your gear before race day, I related my Ultra-Trail du Mont Blanc mishap in 2011 involving a poor gear choice. As mentioned, I had regrettably worn ladies capris, not realizing that they had a special seam running through the crotch. That seemingly innocent seam wasn't noticeable at first, but believe me, by mile 35, I was painfully aware of it. Using my hands and eventually a ziplock bag as barriers down below allowed me to hobble to the 50-mile aid station, whereupon I searched out some different clothing and lubrication. I ended up finishing the race, but having been utterly taken out of my game, I was 20 hours behind the winner. In that instance, chafing cost me my competitive finish in a big race.

You likely already know where your chafing hot spots are. Apply an ample layer of lubricant such as Bodyglide to those high-friction spots before your race. If you are thorough with it at the race start, you should not need to reapply, but make sure your crew has some on hand and do reapply later if needed.

If nipples are your hot spot, as they are for many male runners, you no longer are stuck with duct tape as your only solution. Running companies have come to the rescue with nipple guards, which are easy to put on and will stay put.

For those who chafe in the thigh and nether regions, compression shorts are your best friend. Wear them preventively, or keep them in a drop bag so that you will have them to change into if needed.

## Should I **shave?**

Shaving is a question of personal preference more than anything else. Runners who frequently use a lot of taping for structural support around their knees or ankles often find it easier if they are shaved. Others feel that applying antichafing products is easier if you don't have to work around a bunch of hair. Shaving is also appreciated by massage therapists, who find it much easier to get a smooth rub on hairless legs. Finally, some runners shave proactively, finding it easier to clean wounds if they fall.

Unlike in swimming, shaving in running is certainly *not* about adding speed. It is mainly for preventive reasons, not performance-based ones, although some runners get a mental bump-up from a pre-race ritualistic leg shaving.

If, despite your best efforts, you do find yourself chafing, try your best to keep salt out of the wound by drying off your perspiration as much as possible and changing into dry clothes when you can.

## Rolled Ankle

The majority of ultras take place on trails, with varied, challenging topography. While trails can make for staggeringly beautiful runs, it is easy to roll an ankle as one traverses the technical, rough, or unfamiliar terrain.

Does a rolled ankle mean the end of your race? Possibly, but perhaps not. Step one after rolling an ankle is damage control. Can you still bear weight on that side? If you have excruciating ankle or foot pain with weight, you may have a broken bone that needs immediate attention. Use a willing shoulder or a stick-crutch to help you to the next aid station or pickup point, elevate your leg above your heart, and apply ice to the area on your way to urgent care to get an X-ray.

If you can still bear weight somewhat comfortably, great! Next step: Did you hear a pop? Sometimes that pop is only the sound of joint movements, one bone knocking against another, or a tendon movement. However, a pop can also indicate a torn tendon or ligament, or a bone breaking. Can you still walk or run? If so, continue slowly until the feeling shakes off and the ankle feels stable enough to endure faster speeds. Monitor swelling, and at the next aid station you can use an elastic bandage such as an Ace wrap from the forefoot to above the bony parts of the ankle to keep the swelling down, or have an experienced medic tape the ankle. If your ankle does not swell but feels unstable, wrapping it with an elastic bandage may also be beneficial. Take care not to wrap the bandage too tightly; a solid rule of thumb is never more than

40 percent of its stretching ability. At the aid station you then need to decide whether you can manage the rest of the race on your injury or need to call it quits. If continuing on the injury is going to cause more damage or limit your future running, then it's probably not worth it.

I remember a 100-mile race in which I rolled an ankle at mile 50 and opted not to continue. In that case, I knew immediately that the roll was severe and that continuing the pounding on the injury could cause long-term damage. In other instances, I've had a roll early on in a race and was able to continue without significant problems. Much depends on where you are in the race, how close you are to finishing, and the estimated long-term effects.

## KINESIOLOGY **TAPE**

Kinesiology tape is used preventively as well as for treating injuries. You have probably seen a lot of kinesiology tape if you've watched beach volleyball or been around the growing number of runners who use it on their legs. Often bright and applied in some rather creative patterns, the tape stabilizes and supports your muscles, helps to treat pain, and even improves proprioception because it stimulates muscle awareness through the subtle, non-restrictive sense of touch. It can help your body help itself, either sustaining you through ultra training or getting you across the finish line on race day.

While the initial application is best done by a health care practitioner, online sources such as YouTube videos can be quite instructive. However, my recommendation is to defer to the professional expertise of a physical therapist or chiropractor.

Remember, a rolled ankle can affect your running form. The rest of the body will compensate to avoid pain, and this may cause more problems.

### Cuts and Bruising

Generally speaking, scrapes and cuts are par for the course (literally) and for the most part can be ignored. Clean off the blood with a wipe or some antiseptic and make a quick assessment of the damage done. Cover the wound as necessary, although between sweat and movement, a bandage is likely to fall off. It should go without saying that if you are bleeding from the head or if blood is flowing heavily from any part of your body, you need to monitor the situation closely and very likely get off the course.

Bruising indicates a pooling of blood beneath the skin. Bruises can result from minor trauma, such as a fall or swipe against a rock, or be an indication of something more foreboding. My good friend ultrarunner Tim Olsen noticed bruising during his winning Western States 100 run in 2013; it turned out that the bruising he was experiencing resulted from his tearing of the muscles that attach at the knee. Blood had begun to pool internally, and at that point he ran the risk of injuring more than his legs; blood clots can cause pulmonary embolisms.

Ask yourself: How bad is the pain? Is the swelling rapidly accelerating? Is a wound clotting?

## TUMMY TROUBLES

Even if you do not normally struggle with a sensitive stomach, you may find yourself dealing with stomach issues on race day. The unique high-voltage cocktail of nerves and soaring adrenaline can cause anxiety and upset the stomach. Add to that the fact that you are running 50 or 100 miles, and you are looking at a high likelihood of at least some tummy troubles.

## PAIN RELIEVERS

Pain relievers might ease discomfort or offer a helping hand at a low point in the race, but they should be approached with caution. Most studies point to NSAIDs (nonsteroidal anti-inflammatory drugs) such as ibuprofen—or "vitamin I," as it is affectionately called among ultrarunners—as being a poor choice of pain reliever during a race. For one, it can mask the muscle damage you are inflicting. Also, studies indicate it can contribute to a condition called rhabdomyolysis, which can result in renal failure (see discussion of kidney failure below).[*]

Aspirin, aspirin creams, naproxen, and acetaminophen, on the other hand, do not present similar problems for the kidneys and are generally good go-to choices for pain relief. I apply an aspirin cream preventively to my calves and around my knees prior to an event because I have found it helps reduce inflammation and manage pain. I might take a single acetaminophen during a race, at mile 50 or so, to obtain a degree of relief when I need it most. However, I limit my intake to just that one. That may be excessively conservative but, personally speaking, I just don't want to rely on it. I am uncomfortable with the idea of masking pain, perhaps running myself into the ground with an injury. Sometimes, when the analgesic wears off later, you make the unpleasant discovery that you would have been better off listening to your body instead of muting its signals! Thus, I recommend a conservative approach to pain relievers.

---

[*] Tamara Hew-Butler and Marty Hoffman, "Running, Rhabdomyolosis, and Renal Failure—Who's at Risk," *UltraRunning*, November 24, 2013.

As a preventive measure, I take an over-the-counter antacid an hour before the race start. This neutralizes acids and staves off heartburn, something I find tends to creep up during long races. Friends use other options, including prescription medications that actually shut off the acid pump in the stomach. I'm not a fan of that approach because when the pump comes back on, it can actually double the amount of acid it produces, leading to more problems.

The antacid is effective for 12 to 24 hours. However, if during a race I find my stomach upset, I always have a Tums or Rolaids at the ready. Many aid stations will have these, as well, but if you are prone to such discomfort, carry them yourself or make sure your crew has some available.

## Vomiting

Several years ago, the North Face ran an ad campaign that I'll never forget. The ad featured my good friend Joe Kulak, USATF Ultrarunner of the Year 2006 and nicknamed "Puking Joe." In the ad, he is midway through a 100-miler with his head buried in a trash can. That ad resonated with me, and probably with anyone who has ever run an ultra. The thing is, vomiting is almost de rigueur in an ultra. You know going into it that it's going to hurt, the ad seems to say, so hey, consider vomiting a badge of honor! An early mentor of mine, top ultrarunner Ann Trason, once famously exclaimed that it wasn't a race until she threw up.

Be prepared for the possibility of vomiting, and don't let it undermine your confidence—or your fueling and hydrating. You may not feel like it, but you must continue to try to eat and drink. Turn to the types of food and drink that comfort you when you are sick—bland foods such as nonacidic fruit (bananas, watermelon,

and peaches), saltines, and bread. Coke or Sprite with a little car-
bonation is always nice, too; some runners find the bubbles cause
them to belch deeply enough that they can release pressure, in much
the same way a plunger works with a clog in a drain. Not eating and
drinking may feel more comfortable when your stomach is upset,
but remember that you absolutely must keep fueling in order to get
through the race. Be conscious of it and conscientious about it.

On the bright side, once you vomit, you will probably feel much
better. Hopefully this will happen only once or twice, and then you
can begin to can get more fluids in and keep them there. Throw up,
move on. Make that your mantra.

For me, the Leadville 100 was the race where nausea and vomiting always reared their ugly heads. Something about that incredibly potent combination of heat, dry air, and altitude got me every
time. And it seemed like no matter what I did to prepare for or
prevent it, I always vomited during that race. One year I was not
even able to finish Leadville as a direct result of my vomiting.

Here's how it often goes down: Mentally you know you must
stay on top of drinking, especially because you are losing so much
water through repeated sweating and cooling. You also know you
must continue to eat, replacing your glycogen stores; however, altitude suppresses your appetite. Once you don't eat, that in and of
itself can make you feel worn out and sick, and then the last thing
you want to do is put anything in your stomach. You continue to
lose energy, becoming more depleted. Sometimes that hollow, nau-
seous feeling develops not because you have put something bad or
upsetting into your stomach but because you haven't put *enough*
into your stomach. That can be tricky to figure out. But if you can't
get it in check, eventually your body will give up on you.

## Why do I feel sick, and **how do I deal with it during a race?**

Nausea and vomiting during an ultra can have several causes: dehydration, heat, running too hard, anxiety, altitude, eating and drinking while running, or eating and drinking the wrong things. Depending on the cause, there are practical solutions for the fix. Try the following:

- Walk when ingesting food or drink.
- Look for warm broth at the aid station—it can soothe an upset stomach.
- Slow down your overall pace.
- Pop a chewable antacid.
- Take food with you, and spread out your consumption over a mile or two.
- Do not use gels until late in the race.
- Avoid drink mixes that are likely to upset your stomach.
- Avoid exotic local foods when racing in foreign lands.

Another common reason for nausea is the sports drink offered at aid stations. Some of the drink mixes available in races use high-fructose corn syrup and many complex ingredients and a low percentage of sodium and other electrolytes. These concoctions, especially if they are ones to which your stomach is unaccustomed, can have deleterious effects on your digestive tract. All drink mixes are not created equal when it comes to their ability to get fluid delivered from your mouth, through your stomach, and into your working muscles. Find out ahead of time what the race will have on the course, and if it is a drink that doesn't work well in your system, be sure to carry your own mix or just drink water and carry salt tablets.

## Diarrhea

Loose, watery stools are a common runner's ailment and can be your nemesis on race day. If you can't get a handle on diarrhea, its draining effects on your body can end your race. So take it seriously and try your best to keep it from happening altogether.

Rule one: Do not introduce a new nutrition plan, either on race day or during the week leading up to it. Some folks go so far as not eating any solid food the day before the race. I find that extreme; if you have trained with solid food, go ahead and continue to eat solid food. As with everything leading up to race day, whatever has been your MO, stay with it. Don't make a last-minute change that takes your digestive system by surprise.

Traveling, particularly to a race in another country, can make sticking with a fueling routine and plan more challenging. Prepare for known sensitivities or preferences by packing accordingly. If you are headed to the middle of Idaho from New York, don't expect to find the same kind of bagel you always eat on race day morning. Plan accordingly.

Pre-race pasta dinners can be a real problem, as can meals at the local restaurant that may not serve the type of food that is best before an ultra. Many runners bring their own food to eat before a race and save the local tasting for after they've completed the task for which they have trained so diligently. It isn't rude to be cautious, especially when it means having a better race and avoiding the ugly side of runner's trots.

If you have experienced diarrhea on prior runs or in races, be sure to keep an antidiarrheal such as Pepto-Bismol on you or with your crew. I cannot emphasize enough how crucial it is to get diarrhea in check during a race.

## KIDNEY FAILURE

Ultras, for many, are synonymous with extreme: extreme distance, extreme heat or cold, extreme terrain, extreme exertion, extreme altitude. It is not hard to see how easy it is, then, to become dehydrated or exhausted. And despite your best efforts, these states are nearly unavoidable. In an event such as Western States or Badwater, for example, nearly everyone is going through dehydration to some degree. Put it this way: If you were to go to the hospital with the hydration levels that most people are functioning at around mile 50 of the Hardrock 100, you likely would be admitted. So it becomes a question not so much of *avoiding* dehydration as of *managing* it as best you can.

In a dehydrated state, when you don't have enough water in your system, the kidneys start processing blood to get even more water out of the bloodstream. Ibuprofen can add to the problem, allowing you to beat yourself up much more than you otherwise would, and allowing for a greater than normal amount of muscle breakdown. Ibuprofen acts as a glue when it gets in the kidneys, and the combination of broken-down blood cells and ibuprofen ceases normal functioning. That is why those affected will stop urinating altogether and begin to take on water in massive quantities.

One indication of a possible developing kidney problem is urine color. As dehydration progresses, urine darkens and can become almost coffee colored. At that point, another indication may be noted, which is that you go from losing weight to instead *gaining* weight because your body is no longer successfully processing fluids. If you check your weight at an aid station, and you've gone from a 5-pound loss to a 10-pound gain, you are in dangerous territory. Other signs of kidney stress include pain when you urinate or back discomfort from the area around your kidneys. The latter starts as an ache but worsens over time. You may also experience vomiting and be unable to keep down any liquid or food.

To avoid getting into a dire situation, endeavor to focus on staying hydrated a full week before an event. Drink conscientiously all week long, during and between meals. The expression "clear and copious" should be your mantra, and don't worry about putting on a few pounds of water weight because it will help you in your race and be gone quickly.

On race day, stay on top of consuming 16 to 24 ounces of fluids per hour in the event. Do not lose track of time and forget to drink or, worse, think you can push through. Heat is a huge factor, as you will lose even more water if temperatures are high. Most important, listen to the signals from your body all along the way; that may be your greatest asset and the best skill you can have going into an ultra.

If you are unable to stay on top of fluids, slow your pace, walking or power hiking as you drink. However, the hard truth is that once you are dehydrated, it is very difficult to come around on that front, short of getting an IV to put fluids straight into your bloodstream. At mile 90 during Western States one year, I became so badly dehydrated that I had to drop out. It was excruciating to stop with only 10 miles to go, but at that point I felt I was dangerously far gone, and nothing was worth risking serious damage.

## HYPONATREMIA

With today's hydration packs holding up to 100 ounces combined with the ease of carrying well-designed handhelds, you can actually carry more water than you can (or should) physically consume. A person can typically handle 20 to 24 ounces of liquid per hour of exercise. However, thanks to great gear, we have the ability to carry far more than that, and this, combined with the fear that we aren't drinking enough, can result in serious overkill. Water is undeniably a lifesaver, but drinking more of it than you need can actually dilute the electrolytes in your body to an unsafe level. If you don't replace those electrolytes, you are at risk for hyponatremia, a dangerous condition in which the salt in your blood is lower than normal levels.

Be sure that the electrolyte replacement fluids you are drinking contain a high enough salt content to avoid hyponatremia. The symptoms of mild hyponatremia are somewhat subtle—an altered gait, reduced focus, and increased falling—and can sneak up on you. Once your blood sodium level drops below the level of mild hyponatremia, you may suffer nausea, vomiting, headache, loss of appetite, weakness, irritability, cramps, seizures, spasms, decreased consciousness, and even a coma. The severity will depend on the speed at which your salt level falls and how diluted it becomes.

To avoid this problem, have a plan. For example, carry water, but at aid stations always plan to supplement with an electrolyte drink. Or carry two handhelds, one with water and one with electrolytes, and alternate drinking from each. (Another benefit of certain electrolyte replacement drinks is that they can be a source of much-needed calories, discussed in more detail in Chapter 3.)

## CRAMPING

Ultrarunners commonly experience a few kinds of cramping. One is a cramping in your side, often called a stitch, that is associated with a quicker pace, running with a full stomach, or GI irritation. Controlled breathing is an effective way to ease this kind of cramping, which is often associated with the shallow breathing that occurs when you pick up the pace. Avoiding hard running on a stomach full of liquid or food is another remedy.

Another typical cramping for ultrarunners is muscle cramping in the calf or quad, often due to fatigue or an imbalance of water, salt, and other minerals. If you have ever had one of these cramps, you know that it can stop you dead in your tracks. Chewable antacid tablets that contain calcium can bring relief by helping to restore electrolyte balance. These can be used preventively, working on stomach problems and also delivering a lot of added benefits for muscle cramps.

## Am I **racing too much?**

I'm often asked this question, and my answer is usually some shade of the following: If you're asking the question, then you are probably doing too much. I do not mean that flippantly or facetiously; I mean that when what you are doing is clearly getting in the way of doing everything else, which often is what leads you to ask this question in the first place, then your racing may be out of balance with other parts of your life. This can be the case not only from the standpoint of the time commitment involved but also from the standpoint of proper health and recovery. Taking care of yourself is an important part of training.

I was once what you might call addicted to running and racing. At age 24, I was working in a menial job that was not my passion. Every day, I looked forward to one thing: training. I trained all the time. It was great because at that time in my life, training and racing didn't get in the way of other things. There were no other things. I was able to train and focus and race with abandon. And that is what I did.

But as life grew more complex, with deeper relationships and a busier, more satisfying career, I had to weigh my aspirations against what was beginning to feel like too much. This meant being choosier about which races I ran.

As ultrarunners, we want to run all of the races! That's part of an ultrarunner's mind-set. But it can become exhausting. In those early days, my goal was simply to run and to be with friends while I did it, and that is how I spent my days and weekends. There's nothing wrong with that, provided (and this is important) you are sleeping well and your performance in training and at races is not diminished.

Unquestionably, from a racing and performance point of view, if you wish to achieve your best or arrive healthy and strong at the start line of your A race, there is no doubt that you will sacrifice that by doing, say, five smaller races leading up to it. Picking and choosing, in this case, is better.

The benefits of running are numerous, and the high associated with it causes us to crave it. And if a little is good, a lot must be great, right?

Continues

Continued

It is easy to fill your day with running and your weekends with racing, but you can wear yourself out. And once you get to the point of overtraining and doing too many races, it can be a long road back. There have been too many successful ultrarunners who found their health jeopardized after racing numerous ultras and haven't found the confidence to return to the sport. Adrenal systems get compromised, sleep schedules become unreliable, and recovery is stymied; mentally the drive to train long miles becomes overwhelming, and burnout is not easily reversible. And, of course, overdoing it is a recipe for overuse injuries. So check in with yourself: Are you able to sleep? Do you find joy in thinking about that next outing? Are you able to get up in the morning for a training run, or are you just barely making it through the week and pushing yourself to an event on the weekend?

Racing is supposed to be fun, and the challenge of an ultra is a marvelous achievement, both mentally and physically. Take the time to revel in that and recover before moving on to the next race.

# 6

# DEALING WITH
## YOUR
## ENVIRONMENT

≡

FEW ULTRAS ARE HELD IN URBAN ENVIRONMENTS; THE VAST majority of routes run through natural settings where the scenery helps inspire you across the distance. Although many runners have a deep affection for wilderness, they are not necessarily versed in what it's like to be deep within it for many hours. Being prepared for wildlife encounters, knowing how to purify water, and getting comfortable on challenging terrain such as ice, snow, mud, and technical trail are crucial tools in your ultra toolbox. Similarly, it is invaluable to be able to handle running in cold conditions, to know how to deal with hot temperatures and how best to cope with running at higher elevations or at night, and, most important, to know how to stay found out there (that is, unless you are mastering the finer details of going to the bathroom in the woods).

## TECHNICAL VERSUS NONTECHNICAL TRAIL

In descriptions of a trail or event, the term "technical" is often tossed around, but what does it mean exactly? Does it mean rocky? Steep? Overgrown? It can mean all of those things—or something else altogether. The truth is that everything is relative for the runner, depending on what he or she is used to, so what one runner calls a technical trail may not be categorized as such by another. The definitions here are strictly my own ideas of what is and isn't technical.

If I can see dirt on more than 25 percent of the path in front of me, then the trail, at that point anyway, is not what I would call technical. For me, trails become technical when they are about 75 percent rocks or roots. But not all rocks or roots are created equal. Are you running over rounded rock, affixed to ground? Not so technical. Jagged rocks lying loose on top of the trail? Technical. Similarly, going off trail, or through scree or shale, can quickly become pretty technical. And if you find yourself climbing over large, craggy rocks? Yeah, you're in technical terrain. And have you ever tried to run on moss-covered or slimy tropical roots? Now there's a serious technical challenge.

When classifying events, generally speaking, if more than 50 percent of a race is on technical terrain, the race itself might be labeled a technical race. The Zane Grey 50 is considered one of the more technical races in the United States because well over half of the course is uneven, involving treacherous footing. In the Zane, you will find yourself running much less on dirt than on other surfaces—thus the deserved technical classification. The Hardrock 100 is classified as highly technical due to its steepness, long climbs, and altitude. The Rocky Raccoon, in contrast, is considered one of the faster, easier 100-milers because it is flat and has so much dirt road. However, don't assume this means there are no technical difficulties. Like many ultras, the Rocky Raccoon also has sections where you may find yourself running through washed-out trail and jumping over roots and rocks. Don't be surprised to encounter sections you might find technical, even if the overall race has not been designated as such. For many, this becomes the most enjoyable and memorable part of the course.

## RUNNING IN MUD

Running in mud can present a few unpleasant challenges. Thick mud can pack into the bottoms of your shoes, adding what feels like a ton of extra weight. A gunked-up bottom means significant loss of traction, as well. Finally, as you tire, dredging through mud can lead to muscle strains, cramps, and pulls as the tackiness of the mud causes you to stride differently and exert your fatigued and electrolyte-depleted muscles.

Your pace and stride are going to slow and change in mud. Be prepared to be on all fours on a muddy incline, if necessary, using your hands to get traction. Try to stomp off as much mud as possible or wipe off what you can on a rock. Many trail running shoes have self-cleaning soles, making them more effective at shedding mud than road shoes. Some trail shoes, however, actually hold on to mud, depending on the outsole pattern, the depth of the lugs, and the particular mud type. Certain clay will stick to any shoe, regardless of the sole surface. When you buy your shoes, it pays to inquire specifically about their various features to ensure you are getting what you want.

Getting dirty is a part of trail racing. Embrace it if you can. The North Face championships in 2012 turned out to be a mud bowl of epic proportions. Some runners were completely defeated by it. Watching them slog through the course, you could see they had no motivation, no momentum. For them, the course was miserable and went on forever. Others, however, ran through it like kids playing in mud puddles, embracing it and having a good time with it. Same conditions, different attitude—and most likely different end result, too. Yes, mud can be frustrating, but staying positive will get you through the course in better fashion and likely at a faster pace. Remember, it's just another variable to hurdle! Roads are predictable. That's why we love trails, right?

## RUNNING ON ICE

The best solutions for confronting icy conditions are hobnails, which are screws you put into your outsoles, carbide-spiked trail shoes, and MICROspikes, removable minimal crampons that bite into the ice. I favor MICROspikes because they can be quickly slid on over your shoe when conditions get dicey and then easily removed when you are on firmer ground, and they are also light, efficient, and pretty easy to carry. There are other types of traction devices, such as traction cleats that are based on a spring system rather than teeth, that are good for walking and hiking. They are not as effective in running, however, because the spring can snap under the greater weight and impact.

Good technique on ice includes being very focused; taking shorter, faster, lighter strides with a wider stance for better balance; having your hands as free as possible; and slowing your pace appropriately for the conditions.

## RUNNING IN SNOW

The first thing to remember about snow is that it has many different personalities. It can be soft and powdery, heavy and wet, or hard packed, with each type creating its own potential hazard. Running in wintry weather means you can be enjoying an easy day, glissading down a peak, for example, and the next thing you know you are on rock-hard ice! This abrupt change presents a dangerous situation, so be familiar with what you are running on and remain alert to temperatures and terrain changes.

When you head out in snow, stay protected from the elements as best you can. Cold and its more menacing partner in crime, frostbite, can end a run quickly. Staying protected means having full coverage from your feet on up. It is common to break through the upper crust of older snow only to ram your shins into the hard surface and cut yourself. Because of this, capris aren't a wise choice when the course is likely to cross through snowfields; go with tights or pants instead. Also, wear higher socks, which can go over or under tights and provide much-needed insulation on your ankles, where abrasion, exposure, and frostbite are common. Further, toe socks are a potentially hazardous choice in the cold; better to allow for the heat that grouped toes create. Wear wool and technical materials, not cotton, which will chill you when it gets soggy.

As for shoes, regular shoes and wool or at least wicking socks are probably all you will need, especially in dry, light snow. In heavy, wet snow, Gore-Tex shoes can provide waterproof protection, but they can also trap water inside, adding weight and creating an unpleasant feeling, as well increasing your susceptibility to blisters. Regarding the outsole, some rubbers are better than others in snow. If you are running in a lot of snow, the main thing to look for is an aggressive tread; this helps with confidence and keeping you upright.

I like to dress in layers, such as a long-sleeved shirt coupled with a vest that covers my core but allows unrestricted arm movement. I really like wool tops, which are great insulators; wool is a natural fiber and a warm option that also works well to wick moisture as the temperature rises. These days, with advances in technical materials, you can get away with a stand-alone piece more than you used to, saving you from the need for multiple layers and having a bunch of extra clothes to deal with as you warm up.

A hat is a must: It covers your ears, an area sensitive to frostbite, and keeps you from losing heat through your head. Gloves or mittens for your hands are also essential. Gloves are a practical choice because they allow you to tie your shoes, get into zippered pockets, adjust your audio, and so on. However, mittens pool the warmth of your whole hand and are a better choice if you are concerned about frostbite. Fortunately, there are convertible mitts, which provide the dexterity of a glove with the warmth of a mitten, as a great hybrid option.

## WATER CROSSING

As a trail runner, sooner or later you are going to have wet feet. There's no way around it. I've seen runners go to great lengths to avoid getting wet—readers, I have even been this runner—but it is fruitless and a wasted effort to boot. If you are wearing synthetic socks and shoes that drain well (which you should be), you will be just fine. Don't waste time finding ways around water. For all you know, you will squander time picking your way around one large puddle, and a quarter mile farther along you'll encounter a larger one you can't get around. So much for staying dry!

In one of my first Colorado races, a group of us were running in the Collegiate Peaks Trail Run when we came upon a flooded dirt road. For a second, we all stood there, assessing, reluctant to go in. I remember I began tiptoeing around it, a little like a cat, when suddenly a runner came up behind us and ran directly through the middle of it, spraying water everywhere. After that, I learned to take on water boldly and with conviction.

Races such as Western States and the Hardrock 100 have notorious water crossings. Look out especially for slick, wet rocks, which can put you on your backside. If the conditions look slick, ensure you have good footing, with one foot secure before you lead off and place your other foot. Have both hands free in larger water crossings, both for balance and so that if you fall, you can put your hands out to hopefully ease your landing.

If the water is high or running hard, it is best to chain up with other runners and ford it together. If you are alone, try searching the bank for a better place to cross. I've searched as much as a mile to find a narrowing or a midway sandbar.

Finally, although your socks should dry quickly, for the sake of comfort, carry an extra pair with you in a waterproof bag or leave them in an appropriately placed drop bag. Even if you don't need to change your socks after all, they make great mittens in a pinch.

## RUNNING AT ALTITUDE

Some great ultra races are run high on mountain trails. It's an aspect that many of us love about them; accordingly, handling altitude becomes a concomitant component of ultra racing.

"Altitude" means, in essence, anything higher than where you are living or than the level to which you have acclimated. Altitude affects every person differently. Denver, which is just over 5,000 feet, can affect some visitors, while I find that I don't feel the affects of altitude until about 8,000 feet. (Perhaps this is a by-product of having been raised in Colorado, spending years running and training there; I can't say for certain.) If you are tired, dehydrated, or otherwise not at 100 percent, you may be more affected by altitude.

### TIPS FOR BETTER **BREATHING AT ALTITUDE**

- Peppermint candy or oil opens up nasal passages, allowing more air in, as do nasal strips.

- Concentrate on rhythmic breathing rather than gasping. It will allow more even breathing and go a long way toward keeping you calm.

- Remove your pack if possible, leaving it with your crew and getting it back later. (Make sure this is allowed by race rules.)

- If you can't ditch your pack, loosen it around your chest and abdomen so that it hangs loose as you hike.

- Use poles to keep yourself upright; this helps open your rib cage, allowing more air to enter and giving your lungs the most capacity.

Can altitude make or break a race? Let's just say that I have run Leadville five times—and finished only twice. The two times that I finished, I was already living in Colorado and went up to Leadville early to train. While there were many other factors in play, to me this is compelling on-the-ground proof that altitude can be a significant player in your race.

A key question to ask yourself is how long will you be at altitude during your race. Will you be climbing one 7,000-foot peak, then quickly coming back down again, or does the race itself start at a challenging altitude and remain there? The John Muir Trail includes several 12,000-feet passes and one that is 13,000 feet. During my fastest known time run on that trail, my partner and I endeavored to get up and over the big passes as fast as possible. This was quite hard and fatiguing, obviously, but I wanted to reduce as much as possible the time spent at altitude because I know the havoc it wreaks on my mind and body.

To prepare, elites often spend several weeks at or above the altitude at which they will be racing, training on the very trails they will run. While you may not have the luxury of spending weeks in your race location, you can take some proactive steps to prepare yourself for leaping the hurdles of altitude.

If you have higher-altitude access in your area or are able to travel to higher elevation, train on it, at least once. Although spending some time at altitude, even if only briefly during training, will not be sufficient for thorough acclimatization, it *will* set you up psychologically for how you will feel at altitude. Just knowing how your body and your mental functions respond, and having the time to test your stomach as you eat and drink at altitude, provides helpful information that can minimize race day surprises and anxiety.

Most runners arrive the day before the start. Although it may sound counterintuitive, arriving the day before is actually preferable to arriving 3 to 5 days before. Why? Because soon after arrival, the body begins a process of acclimatizing to altitude by producing red blood cells to replace those lost due to reduced oxygen in the air. This process at first takes the body on a downward cycle as it works to adjust before it eventually replaces those cells and produces even more to help you handle the new elevation. Acclimatization happens over a period of 3 to 4 weeks (although full acclimatization takes far

## ALTITUDE **SICKNESS**

Major signs of altitude sickness include shortness of breath, headaches, light-headedness, and upset stomach. Watch your heart rate; should it get very high or irregular, you may be dealing with a more serious altitude problem. Getting down out of altitude as quickly as possible is the best way to lower your heart rate.

Drink mixes and pills intended for use at high altitudes are options to mitigate altitude sickness, but these are designed simply to allow you to function, not to help you compete. Studies suggest that Viagra can be a useful resource because it targets smooth muscle tissue, allowing blood flow to increase across the board, and can be a performance enhancer. More natural approaches include chewing on natural licorice, which can open up your bloodstream and speed your heart rate.

Stay on top of your hydration. You will find that you go through everything—food, water, oxygen—much faster at altitude, so stay on top of it. And altitude can wreak havoc on the GI tract, so try not to eat heavy meals near to or during the race.

longer). If you arrive a few days before the start in the hopes of acclimatizing, you are giving your body a chance to begin the process, but you will find yourself with a still-reduced cell count on race day and a fatigued body that has been working overtime to adjust. This can leave you low on energy and stamina just when you need it most. If instead you show up the day before the race, very little adjustment will have taken place, with fewer blood cells lost.

If you have access to an altitude tent, you can speed up the process of becoming acclimated, but that is not the case for most recreational runners. Most runners need to find ways to deal with it on the fly.

## LIGHTNING

In areas of high altitude, such as the Colorado high country, you will commonly find yourself running above the tree line. While this is a breathtaking place to run, storms, particularly in the summer, are common. Above the tree line, you are completely exposed and therefore more at risk for being struck by lightning. Rule one, therefore, is to be proactive with your training plans. In plotting your day's run, for example, plan to start early enough to ensure you will be off any summits before noon due to the high potential for afternoon storms.

Sometimes Mother Nature surprises, however, upending your best-laid plans. So if lightning strikes while you are above the tree line, get as low to the ground as possible as quickly as possible. If you can get back into the trees, do so (not, however, sheltering beneath or against one because trees are commonly struck by lightning).

If you cannot get to shelter and have no choice but to remain exposed, your goal is to get as low as possible without delay. I have been on mountaintops and felt my hair standing on end; this was way too close for comfort, and I hit the ground immediately. Sheltering in a dugout, behind a pile of rocks, or under a large rock is ideal. Stay away from water sources, which attract lightning. Also, if you've got trekking poles, I'd suggest ditching them; in any case, do not have them sticking out of your pack because they will serve as lightning rods.

Take thunder seriously as a warning sign. Thunder typically accompanies lightning, so if you hear thunder rumbling as you are preparing to head up into the mountains, rethink your plans. Think of thunder as nature's emergency broadcast system, cuing you to get out of exposed areas before things go bad. Revise your training plan or end your run. It is definitely not worth it to try to push up over that next summit. Races have been suspended for lightning. It is not something to mess with.

## COLD/HEAT MANAGEMENT

### Cold

- Come prepared with everything you may need, using drop bags or layering on your person as is practical.
- Dressing in layers is key. Today, technical materials and clothing are so thin and lightweight, there is no excuse for not carrying them along with you if you know you may be facing cold conditions. Calf or arm sleeves are a great option for added warmth and are easily removed.
- Dehydration can lead to getting too cold, so stay on top of your hydration.
- Make sure you are getting warm liquids to help warm your core. Many aid stations will have soup or oatmeal available.

- Make sure you have hats, gloves, and extra socks (wool). Even if you don't have to replace the socks you are wearing, the extra ones make handy mitts if you need them.
- Do your due diligence: At what point in the race might you need items such as a hat or parka? Plan accordingly.
- Never underestimate nighttime temperature swings, especially at altitude. Also, if you end up having to walk or stop, that's when you get the coldest. The heat you were generating while running gets lost, and you can go into a hypothermic state, especially if your base layers are wet from sweat. So if you encounter large drops in temperature, make sure that you keep moving to generate heat, even accentuating movements more than you otherwise would.

## HYPOTHERMIA

Hypothermia occurs when the body's core temperature drops so low that the body loses its ability to manage its temperature. It usually occurs as a result of external circumstances, such as a drop in outside temperature combined with insufficient clothing or layers, and then can become compounded if you are not taking in enough fluids or nutrition to help combat it.

As temperatures drop, you require more calories to stay warm. So you must fuel *beyond* what you need simply to get through the miles; you also must fuel to meet the demands of your environment. To make it worse, if your pace falls off or you pause at an aid station, you stop generating heat through running, just when you need it most.

While it takes time to reach a hypothermic state, the symptoms can come on quickly. They include uncontrollable shaking,

Continues

Continued

numb extremities, a feeling of cold that goes all the way to your core, blue lips, and chattering teeth.

Know where you are going to be running and the potential extremes. Be prepared with layers, either in your pack, left in an appropriate drop bag, or held by your crew. I have seen the weather change in an instant at races. At Leadville, which takes place in August, you may find yourself sifting through snow at the top of Hope Pass; for a runner who is unprepared, this could dampen even the heartiest ambitions.

One of my first 100-milers was the Iditasport in Alaska. This race is run along the famed Iditarod Trail as well as frozen lakes and streams. You must navigate snow machines and teams of mushing dogsleds, as well as snow and freezing temps in the mid-February darkness. I had been leading most of the race with another competitor when things took a turn for the worse. I went for a long stretch without water after my hydration pack became clogged with electrolyte drink powder. Although I had taken the necessary precautions to make sure I had insulated tubing, I hastily (and mistakenly) added the mix first instead of my water; this choked my water supply by pushing the mix into the tube.

Because I was afraid of getting lost, I opted to stay close to the runner ahead of me rather than take time to stop and fix my bladder. I'd like to say that was my only error, but, unfortunately, both that runner and I ended up getting lost later on just when I couldn't afford more time out in the elements. To add insult to injury, we ran on unstable frozen water that had pooled above the ice, drenching our shoes and pants. Recipe for disaster? You bet. Without water, without sufficient calories to compensate for getting lost, and now hypothermic, I went from leading the race to barely finishing the next day, after spending some 5 hours in a warming hut.

Aid stations usually have warm liquids and a heat source, such as a fire or heater. If you are not prepared, beware. You can be removed from the race for hypothermia, and rightly so, because it can become a serious health concern if not arrested.

## Heat

- Train in the heat. During my training leading up to notoriously hot events such as Western States or the Javelina Jundred, I'll run during the hottest part of the day. This helps prepare me for the unique feeling of running in the heat.
- Sauna training is a great heat simulator. I do push-ups in the sauna, which mimics how it feels to exert myself in the heat, raising my heart rate as well.
- If you know your race is going to be both hot and humid, and especially if you are coming from a dry climate, use a steam room in lieu of a sauna.

### HEATSTROKE

Under normal circumstances, the body is able to regulate its temperature through mechanisms such as sweating. However, if your body temperature continues to rise, due to exertion in the heat, often combined with insufficient hydration, you are at risk for exhaustion or heatstroke. Problematic signs include high fever, a flushed face, hallucinations, absence of sweating, extreme fatigue, difficult breathing, nausea, headache, confusion, and a high heart rate.

If you suffer these symptoms, slow to a walk in order to drop your heart rate and try to get to a location where the temperature is lower. Cool things off internally by drinking cold fluids or eating ice chips, or submerge yourself in cold water, where possible, to get your core temperature down. Try icing your head, neck, or hands, which sends signals to the brain that you are cooling down. Heatstroke can become life-threatening; remember that your health comes before finishing any race.

- Murphy's Law dictates that your race day will be the hottest day of the year. Expect that; don't be caught by surprise.
- Avoid direct sunlight as much as possible. For example, stay in the shade of the aid station as you address your needs there, and choose the shaded side of the path over the sunny.
- Wear something to cover both your face and your head—a flapped hat over a visor offers protection, cover, and shade.
- Carry ice in your hat. At the blistering Western States 2013, I put ice in my hat at every aid station.
- Keep on top of your fluids, even more than you think necessary.
- Get wet whenever the opportunity presents itself. Cool off in streams, and use sponges or misters when they are available. Doing this takes only a short time, and the relief is well worth it.
- Wear technical fabrics and choose lighter colors. Perhaps counter-intuitively, less clothing is not necessarily better; removing layers

## WHEN YOU HAVE TO GO—A FEW TIPS

- Make sure you are off the trail and as far away as possible from high-traffic areas.
- Watch out for thorns or poison ivy or oak. Make your way to a clearing, if possible.
- Once you go, take the time to cover it. The protocol is to dig a small hole, perhaps with your heel, and bury it.
- Set something alongside the trail before you leave it, such as your backpack or water bottle, so that other people know where you left the trail. Then, if you should fall or lose your way, people will know where to begin looking.

only exposes you further to the sun's direct rays and creates more problems. Instead, block the sun with light clothing, which will keep you cooler than stripping down.

- Holding an ice-cold water bottle will cool your hands, which sends cooling signals to the brain. Fill a bottle with ice at every aid station.
- Take salt. Be sure to read the dosage for the pills you are using. I take two pills per hour during the hottest time of day.

## GOING TO THE BATHROOM

Racing and training for ultras means hours spent outdoors. You are going to have to go to the bathroom at some point, and there will rarely if ever be a proper bathroom nearby. Don't be anxious; everyone has to do it. And, yes, there is a right—or at least a better— way to do it (see sidebar on page 124).

Chafing from urine or waste gone awry happens—once it even cost me a race. So, believe me when I say you do not want copious amounts of urine wetting or soiling the material you are wearing. Although I have heard of a number of runners who wouldn't waste the time to slow down and go, I don't think that is the best approach for all of us. When you feel the urge to go, take the time to do it properly. It's human to want to rush because it might feel odd to be exposed and, well, we are in a race after all. However, it pays to take the care and time to follow the proper process of elimination.

EXPERT **TIP**

Go to the bathroom as close as possible to start time. Drinking coffee can help move things along in the morning so that you can evacuate your bowels before race start. Ultras often start before dawn, so train your body to get used to waking up early, practicing going to sleep early so you can wake easily and do your business in the wee hours.

## ANIMALS

For most of us, running an ultra offers a special opportunity to spend time in the wild, as many ultras are set, at least partly, in remote locations. Training and racing often take place on trails and paths that wind through mountains, forests, or fields, where the likelihood of sharing that space with wild animals is high. This opportunity to be with wildlife is intriguing for some, but it can be a little bit intimidating for others.

Most animals you encounter will only want to get away from you as quickly as possible. However, at an inopportune moment, such as if you encounter a mother bear with cubs or a moose and her calves, there is a chance that an animal might act in an aggressive manner. Most of the time this behavior is merely posturing; do not take that for granted, though, and do take the appropriate precautions. I remember fighting for a podium spot at the Wasatch 100 in Utah when I unexpectedly came upon two moose standing directly on the trail. Moose are notoriously defensive animals, and enormous to boot. Imposing and beautiful as they are, they are also the animals I least want to encounter in the wild. So although I was in something of a hurry, I could do nothing but wait until they chose to move off of the trail. What is a 10-minute delay when it comes to safety?

Remember, while a healthy respect for wild animals is always required, being fearful is unnecessary. We've all heard stories of people encountering animals where the outcome was not desirable. For what it is worth, I've logged a lot of miles in wild, crazy, remote places and have yet to come into contact with an aggressive animal. I've run within 10 yards of mountain lions on a few occasions and have seen dozens of bears and even a few Texans; without fail,

## SAFETY TIPS **IN THE WILD**

- Familiarize yourself with the area. Is it notorious for bear or moose activity, for example?

- Running at certain times increases the possibility of mixing with wildlife. Dusk and early morning are active times for animals. Certain times of the year, for example, mating season, mean more potential for interaction or aggressive animal activity.

- In state parks and many municipalities, trailheads will post up-to-date bulletins on recent animal sightings in the area and will suggest appropriate precautions. Heed these.

- If you know you are going into hot spots for animals, consider carrying pepper spray. The jury is out on how effective it really is, but if it gives you the little bit of peace of mind or the confidence to help you get away, then it might be a good option. Bear spray is effective only in deterring bears under certain circumstances, so you need to be aware that wind, rain, and temperature can reduce its impact, as may your proximity to the animal when it charges.

- Make noise—talking, whistling, or wearing a bell—while you are running to keep from surprising an animal, which can lead to a defensive response. Let animals know you are coming; that gives them time to do what they want, which is usually to get away.

- If confronted, try to make yourself appear bigger. Shake a big stick or rock that makes you seem menacing. Never turn your back and run. This can trigger an animal's predatory instinct.

- The best way to react depends on the situation and the animal. If a bear is aggressive, consider playing dead. If a mountain lion is aggressive, use a loud, deep voice and threatening gestures. For more information on how to handle wildlife encounters, check out the many resources available online or at the bookstore.

---

**SNAKES** ON THE TRAIL

During my time in Colorado and now southern Oregon, rattle-snakes have been a worry. When it is hot or very sunny, they can become a nuisance on your favorite trails. Trouble is, you usually won't see them until you are already stepping on or very close to one. They are often found among the rocks or brush, so if you are going off trail, stay very aware. If one bites you, try to minimize the mobility of the area that was bitten, keeping it below your heart and removing anything that would constrict if there is swelling. You must get to an emergency room to receive antivenom as soon as possible. Time is of the essence.

---

these animals have seemed more afraid of me than I was of them and have wanted nothing to do with me.

## RUNNING WITH DOGS

Dogs make excellent training partners and delightful trail companions. That said, be aware that certain breeds handle the elements and the time on their feet required in ultra training better than others. As with humans, the more your dog trains with you, the more fit it will be. However, some breeds do have limitations, whether it is having short hair that doesn't offer much protection in cold weather or a snub or concave nose that compromises breathing. My dog is an English setter—border collie mix, and she has run many, many miles with me over the years—in her prime, more than 30 miles at a stretch! But as she has aged, I have pulled back on her mileage.

## WATCH OUT FOR **STINGERS**

Bees, wasps, and hornets can range from being a nuisance to a serious problem. Certainly if you are allergic, you must carry your medicine with you in the event that you encounter these insects. Some ultra events will have such meds on hand at the aid station, but if you know your allergy is a problem, do not rely on others to have what you need. Many runners take the precaution of carrying an epinephrine pen.

Follow all signs and requirements for pets, which vary by trail. Remember to use the same etiquette that you would if you were in a city park. Don't abandon your dog's waste just because you are in the great outdoors; carry a bag with you and clean up on the trail and in high-traffic areas such as trailheads. Dogs should be under voice command or on a leash. You must be able to control your dog if wildlife is encountered, whether to prevent your four-legged friend from becoming a meal or to keep your pet from chasing after its own trail snack. You love your dog, but be aware that many people fear dogs or can be unpleasantly surprised by a dog that runs toward them or jumps up. Dogs running free on a singletrack trail can cause tripping hazards for other runners. In a word: Be sensitive.

## GOING OFF TRAIL

In races in the United States, runners are expected to stay on the marked course for the entirety of a race. Deviating in a way that would advance you closer to the finish is grounds for disqualification. If you accidentally find yourself off course, most races will make you go back to the point where you left the trail and restart from that point in order to be considered a legitimate finisher. I remember losing the markings in a race once and finding myself way off course. Although by the time I found the course again I had gone much *farther* than the requirements of the race, I was nevertheless disqualified for missing part of the official course. Lesson? Always backtrack. This is not only the surest way to find the trail if you are lost (see page 131 on getting lost) but also the way to remain in a race's good standing. (Rules in European races differ; often you are allowed to find the quickest point from A to B. Check the rules to be sure.)

It is tempting to cut across switchbacks, but even if no one is there or there is no rule against it, remember that switchbacks not only are created to make the grade easier and more runnable but also work for erosion control. Think about the Leave No Trace ethic and your love for the environment when you consider trying to save a few seconds.

Similarly, while it is tempting to skirt to the side of a muddy trail, please do not. Stepping off trails widens them, converting singletrack into a thruway. For the privilege of racing in remote, delicate, or fragile areas, we must respect the rules or we will lose that opportunity. Be aware, follow signs, and stay on the trail, even if you have to get your feet muddy.

## TRASH ON THE TRAIL

Common sense and respect rule the day. And a simple rule: Whatever you take in, take out. This includes the obvious, such as wrappers and toilet paper, but also organic trash such as banana peels and orange peels. You don't know what animal might eat it or what

problems it may cause. Some regions that you'll be racing in have
different rates for breaking down organic matter, and none of us
want to see that kind of trash out and about on our daily runs.
Foreign matter, even biodegradable, can affect an area more than
you know. One runner I know, who had run dozens of ultras, was
once DQ'd for dropping a banana peel outside an aid station at
Javelina. Respect your environment, and leave it as you found it.

## GETTING LOST

Ultra races differ from road races in several ways, but one notable
distinction is that you can't follow other racers down the road in
the way you can in, say, the Boston Marathon. Indeed, in an ultra
you might not see another person for hours. Race directors try very
hard to mark their courses, particularly areas where doubt might
arise, such as at a fork in the trail, but even the most conscientious
RD can't flag the entire wilderness with confidence ribbons. The
onus is on you, the runner, to have some idea of where you are
heading. Getting lost in a race is frustrating at best and life-
threatening at worst. Take it seriously, because unlike Yogi Berra,
you won't always be able to come to a fork in the road and take it.

Consider the Hardrock 100, a famously majestic race in south-
western Colorado that is difficult to navigate at times. The course
traverses valleys and basins into high alpine meadows and ridges
where course marking and spotting can be difficult. At times your
head is buried in your knees, as you climb thousands of feet at an
already dizzying elevation, topping out more than 14,000 feet above
sea level, and cloudy vision can afflict even the most acclimatized
runner. To successfully complete this race, you need to know, at
least generally, how to get from point A to point B with confidence

under a number of conditions, including at night. This high level of orienteering is a larger part of the Hardrock 100 than of some other ultras, but having that intimate knowledge beforehand will help your momentum in any ultra and keep you from making directional errors when you don't have the energy or wherewithal to think clearly. Personally, I have been lost for 30 minutes or more during Hardrock, with literally no idea what direction I was headed. Flags get knocked over, pikas eat them, or you don't see them. Sometimes tundra grows over the trail, or the trail meanders through a marsh or rock fields, and distinguishing it becomes a challenge.

Hardrock is an extreme example, but the takeaway point for any race is this: Do your due diligence by familiarizing yourself with the course in advance. You will most likely be heading into territory that is strange to you and wilderness and climates that are often harsh; you can lose your bearings quickly. Do not rely on the flagging tied on an occasional shrub or tree to do your orienteering for you.

Sometimes, despite our best efforts, we get lost. Be prepared for that possibility by ensuring you have sufficient food and water. When running and racing, we usually want to carry as little as possible; that's understandable. However, if something unforeseen happens, ask yourself, do I have a little bit extra?

Always have some sort of directional device on you if you aren't able to orienteer by the sun or stars or are in an unfamiliar region. Watches often have this ability, or a small compass can help you find north. Also carry a map of the route. The race web site should include a course map. If possible, print it out (you can reduce it, making it as small as you wish) and carry it along. Many races even have turn-by-turn directions that guide competitors through the course, informing them of where to go at each intersection they confront along the route. Study the route and take responsibility for knowing where you are heading.

During the race, if you are being asked to turn off of the main trail, this turn will likely be marked and may have volunteers in place to direct you. However, as mentioned, ribbons sometimes fall off, flour gets washed away, and volunteers don't always show up for their directing duties, so if you arrive at a fork and are unsure, choose the more traveled path. Often, minor trails will peter out after they leave a main trail; these can appear inviting, but it's best to look for running shoe footprints in the dirt.

The best thing to do if you discover you are lost is to turn around and go back to where you came from. Backtracking can be very frustrating, particularly in a race situation, but trying to find a new path or, worse, thinking you've found a shortcut back to the trail is often the last thing that works. Retracing your steps is the simplest way to get back on track. Don't panic or fret about how much time you've lost. Rather, stay quiet, move slowly, calm down, and listen; your senses can get you out of an area, particularly your hearing. Listen for other runners, which can lead you back to the right place. You may also find yourself in the difficult position of being disqualified for going off course, so taking the time to get back on the trail at the point at which you went wrong is of the utmost importance; most race rules prohibit any variance from the course, even if no time is gained.

## DRINKING FROM NATURAL WATER SOURCES

My first and best advice is probably stating the obvious: Don't drink unfiltered water if you can avoid it. Be prepared with enough water, or if you are intending to drink from a natural water source, have a means to filter that water. While water quality depends on human and animal activity in the area, as well as a few other factors, more often than not you can count on giardia or bacteria living in natural water sources. Drinking infected water won't cause you distress the moment you drink it, or probably even during your run, necessarily, but you can expect to face discomfort and mild to severe GI issues down the line. Avoid this likelihood by bringing your own water or else a filtering device.

When runners are out running, pack space is usually at a premium, and the less weight the better. The lightest, most space-saving water-filtering device is iodine, in the form of tablets or drops. The upside of iodine is that it is easily carried; the downside is the bitter taste of water that has had iodine added, as well as the 30 to 40 minutes of waiting time required as the iodine neutralizes the water. On a recent Rim to Rim to Rim run in the Grand Canyon, I found myself thirsty and wanting to drink snow runoff at the top of the North Rim. Concerned about possible grazing there, I used iodine before consuming the water. While it may have been overly cautious, it was an easy way to ensure I wasn't taking in something I shouldn't.

The SteriPEN is one of the best inventions I've seen in outdoor equipment in years. This small, lightweight wand harnesses ultraviolet rays to purify water in less than a minute for a 16-ounce bottle. One downside is that it requires batteries, so if you are counting on it for your purified water, you should consider toting along extra batteries, depending on how long you will be out and how often you will be sterilizing water.

Another filtration device is a handheld pump, which is also a good option, although far less compact. On the plus side, it acts instantly, which means reduced waiting time for clean water.

As quickly as the pump acts, I confess, on a fastest known time attempt on the John Muir Trail in 2013, my partner and I got dead tired of the process of filtering water. We had underestimated how much water we'd go through over 3 tough days of exertion, as well as how much time it took to filter with a pump. By the last day, I was exhausted and thirsty, so I began taking water straight from the stream. I am not saying I recommend this, but in this case I knew that the waters are relatively clean in the Eastern Sierra, and so even though it had been a dry year with low flow, I took a calculated risk and did not get sick. If you find yourself in a situation in which you have no other option but to drink unfiltered

## DRINKING UNFILTERED WATER—A FEW TIPS

- If the source is a stream, drink from the uphill side.

- Get your water from an area upstream and as far away from the trail as possible, putting distance between you and areas where humans and animals congregate.

- Pull water from a source with flow rather than dipping into water that is stagnant. (That said, shallow standing water in high alpine areas is often drinkable, since the water can be filtered by the sun, as UV filtration usually kills most anything.)

- Other water sources include cacti or natural basins or bowls, such as in a hollowed-out tree, which sometimes collect rainwater.

- If you are lucky enough to be around fruit trees, you can also find ripe apples, peaches, oranges, and other fruit to quench your thirst.

water, then an on-the-ground knowledge of the area can go a long way toward reducing your risk.

## NIGHT RUNNING

Night running divides runners: For some, it's one of the best things about running and training for an ultra; for others, it is the most dreaded aspect. I'm in the former camp. For me, night running opens up the adventure of trail and ultrarunning. It's always just a little bit mysterious to run at night—certainly not something that we human beings do regularly or naturally—and that is what makes it so exciting. If you do not feel that way, however, fear not. Practice and experience *will* help you get more comfortable with running at night. And that's a good thing because many ultra distances will demand some night running. Whether it is running all the way or just partway through the night, or perhaps in the dark of the start line in early morning hours, you will want to make running without natural light if not your best friend, then at least a companion with whom you feel comfortable.

Your best training for night running starts by getting out there and running at night. The more you can get out there and be productive in the dark, the better you will feel about it, and the more confidence you will gain.

Running at night is easier than ever, given the advances in lights and headlamps. Truly, there are lights available to you now that are basically the equivalent of a car headlight. In fact, you can probably see better running on trails today than you could driving a car in the 1990s! These advances open up the whole trail in a way that was not possible a few years ago. (For a more detailed discussion of lights, see Chapter 4.) The brightness of these lights is also a good deterrent to animals, if that is something that concerns you. It is certainly not a rarity to come across the glimmer of animal eyes in the dark. But remember that, while this can be a bit spooky, it is still the case that animals you see normally prefer to stay away from you. This is especially true if you are flashing around a blinding light, which provides ample advance warning of your arrival and, better yet, opportunity for their departure.

## TIPS FOR **RUNNING AT NIGHT**

- Have a good light source.

- Watch for tree branches and other unexpected stumbling blocks on the periphery of your vision. Your light only casts so much of a circle, so try to be doubly aware of your surroundings.

- Don't be a slave to pace; slow down when you need to negotiate tricky, dark areas.

- Temperatures typically drop at night; be sure you are properly dressed and have enough layers.

- Switch out your visor for a beanie, so as not to block your vision any more than necessary.

- Wear your illumination around your waist, so that the light is closer to the ground. And consider carrying a flashlight as well for spotting course markings or exposed roots. A lot of ultra-runners prefer to use two light sources to ease the strain on their eyes and enhance depth perception, pairing a headlamp with a handheld or waist-mounted light.

When I was attempting a fastest known time on the Colorado Trail, I got lost one day, a few hours before sunrise. I remember coming out of the woods into what felt like an open area and being suddenly confronted with dozens of eyes. They not only were staring at me but seemed to be coming my way—rapidly. I had no idea what they belonged to or where to go. Should I try to outrun them? Judging from the sound of rustling limbs and heaving breath, they were coming at an aggressive pace, and so I picked up mine as well, heart beating in my throat. When one made a sound, I finally realized I was running like hell from a herd of cows. I learned later that I was in a pasture where the herd wandered freely, and the farmer would often show up in the early morning hours to feed them. They obviously mistook me for the farmer. Now, I'm not normally afraid of cows, but the combination of the animals' gleaming, mysterious eyes, my own tired mind, and an edginess at being lost in the dark flustered me, to say the least. Holy cow!

Keep in mind that finding your way becomes exponentially harder when it is dark. No matter how many times you've been on your favorite run, it will look different in the dark. It may feel longer or shorter, but it will be different at night. When training for an event, if you can get out and run on the actual course, so much the better, but for many runners this is not practical. Just getting the time in on a dark trail, perhaps running the specific distance and particular hours that you expect to encounter during the event, will be excellent practice for the big day.

As precious ultra training, getting out on the trail for a long run after a busy day will help replicate the reality of running through the night in your event. It's one thing to head out for a night excursion with a clear head and fresh eyes, but that is not likely to be the case in your race. Do not try for performance on your night runs, such as doing a key tempo run. Just getting the mileage in and being out there during the night is the key.

Consider getting a group together to do it; this can ease a lot of the anxiety we tend to have about being alone in the woods at night, and it is also just a lot more fun.

# 7

# **RACE** DAY

NOW THAT YOU KNOW ABOUT TRAINING, TECHNIQUE, GEAR, nutrition, and self-care, it's time to put it all together and test it out with a race. Getting to the start line prepared is the hardest part, but race day presents its own unique challenges and opportunities. To race right, you'll want to be sure you travel to the start line with grace, do a proper warm-up, assemble and brief your crew and pacers, and plan all necessary drop bags. Once the gun goes off, you'll want to stay focused on dialing in your fueling and hydration technique and timing, stay aware of your pace and any cutoff times you may face, hone your mental focus, and flawlessly execute your passing technique. After crossing the finish line, you'll want to be ready with your post-race strategy (which may or may not include beer!).

## TRAVELING TO YOUR RACE

Sleep the night before a race is never quality. You might feel stressed, taking care of last-minute items, or you may have trouble falling asleep due to excitement. The best night's sleep you have is likely to be a couple nights prior, for example, on Thursday night if the race is Saturday. Therefore, consider not traveling on Thursday, if possible. Stay home and take full advantage of that good night's sleep. If traveling on the Thursday is unavoidable, however, then consider leaving as early as possible so that you have plenty of time to arrive and acclimate before bedtime. Don't underestimate the amount of energy you will spend driving a car all day en route to a race or sitting for hours in an airport and a plane. These things require you to be alert and can be surprisingly tiring. Remember, rest includes not just your body but also your brain.

If you are traveling to Europe or from one coast to the other, there is the added issue of jet lag to consider. If you cannot travel early enough to adapt to the new time zone, you can try to mimic the time difference in a few different ways: Go to bed earlier or later the week prior, and eat at times that are appropriate for the race time zone.

For example, even though I normally run in the afternoon—the time of day that my body naturally feels awake and energetic—in the few weeks leading up to Western States, a race that begins at 5:00 a.m., I prepare by getting up early to run. Practice getting up at the hour you'll have to wake on race morning to help your body get used to it, training your digestive system, especially. You'll want to get to the start line as light as possible, and while race nerves may help, you may need to reset your digestive system's clock so that it, too, is ready to go, preferably about 30 to 45 minutes before the scheduled race start so you don't have to rely on port-o-lets.

In sum, help your body adjust. Don't just expect it to perform whenever and however you wish it to at exactly the moment you want—you can't ignore your normal cycles.

## WARMING UP BEFORE THE RACE

Most races start very early, which is already a major adjustment to your normal schedule. Add to that the fact that you probably didn't sleep well the night before your race. "Warming up" in this case really means just getting your body moving, inside and out.

You should eat before the event—enough to feel full—but not too close to the time that you have to run. What does this mean? It means, yes, getting up earlier than you probably want to, eating something, and then returning to bed if you wish. You want to give yourself ample time to eat and digest. This might mean 3 hours before an event or, at a minimum, 1.5 hours. I get up at least a few hours prior to a race to get calories in, via either a bagel or some hearty oatmeal, plus I drink 32 ounces of a sports drink. I may also eat a few chews or a gel, one with caffeine if for some reason I can't get my hands on a hot cup of coffee.

As for a physical warm-up at the start line, for 100 miles, this is not as crucial. Walking around a bit, maybe a half hour before race start, or jogging easily for a few minutes should suffice. For a 50-mile race, consider doing a little bit more, perhaps warming up from where your car is parked, jogging to the start line and back, for

10 minutes, to get the blood going to the right muscles. This will get things moving, allowing you a chance to go to the bathroom, as well. Depending on the temperature, you may need to actually warm your muscles by raising your heart rate, especially if you plan to strip off layers and hit the start line wearing less than is optimal, knowing you'll soon be exerting yourself and possibly sweating.

As for stretching prior to a race, that is not something I choose to do. My muscles are way too tight and do not feel warm enough in those pre-race hours to stretch effectively. Instead, I often take a warm shower before a race to loosen up, which in a more benign way gets the blood flowing. And it is usually quite cool in those predawn hours; just trying to generate some heat at the race start with gentle calisthenics can be an effective warm-up.

## PREPARING YOUR CREW AND PACERS

To use rock star terminology—and why not?—your pacers and crew members are like your handler, focused 100 percent on your needs and providing support to help you meet your goals. They are there for you, but it is your job to help them help you by letting them know clearly and in advance what your goals are and preparing them for what you need to achieve those goals. Sending a detailed e-mail, talking on the phone, and/or meeting in person beforehand is critical. Discuss the challenges of the race and lay out your A, B, and C goals, as well as the pace and time frame required to meet each. Thinking through your needs and expectations in advance and discussing these in detail with your support team mean fewer unknowns on race day.

Bear in mind that technical, vehicular, and navigational difficulties can happen no matter how much you prepare; your crew may fall asleep or not show up where they are supposed to; pacers may

## CHECK **THE RULES**

Many ultra races allow pacers and crew, but the degree to which they can be involved varies. Some races, particularly those under 100 miles, may not allow support at all. Always check the race rules before you start planning.

struggle. Keep things in perspective and keep a level head when fails occur. In the end, you are responsible for yourself. If something happens, be prepared to roll with it as best you can.

## Crew

Loosely defined, your crew is there to supply any aid you require outside of that which is available at an aid station, providing items and care that are customized to your individual race. Think of your crew as your backbone, supporting you logistically, physically, and emotionally to get you to your goal. They will meet you at pre-arranged spots along the route, where they will lay out your needed gear, massage your feet or shoulders if that's what you want, and supply you with fresh batteries, a favorite snack, or much-needed antichafing lotion, maybe before you even ask for it. They will carry backup items, such as a rain jacket and your second-favorite socks; they will make sure you reapply sunscreen because even though you may not notice you are burning, they will. In other words, they will anticipate your needs and keep you moving through the event.

In most ultras, your crew will do a lot of driving and must be able to follow directions and maps. Many racecourses lie outside of cell coverage, so they shouldn't rely on smartphone maps for navigation. They should have a vehicle tough enough for the terrain. To make it to designated meeting spots, they will be driving many miles, through the day and night, and thus should be hardy and prepared for little sleep.

A crew's support extends far beyond the logistical, although that is a crucial part of it; they are also there to supply emotional support. When you have been out running for hours on end, often with few if any other runners around you, it is crucial to have a crew that can build you up. They know and value the effort and dedication you have put into this event and are committed to helping you achieve what you've set out to do.

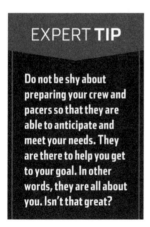

EXPERT **TIP**

Do not be shy about preparing your crew and pacers so that they are able to anticipate and meet your needs. They are there to help you get to your goal. In other words, they are all about you. Isn't that great?

Having been on both sides, I can tell you that crewing can be almost as tiring as running the race! Having a larger crew can aid with some of the fatigue and responsibilities. How many crew members you choose is up to you, but it is ideal to have enough so that everyone finds a time to sleep, eat, and take a turn at driving.

## Pacers

A pacer is a runner who accompanies you in the latter stages of a race, providing encouragement, motivation, support, and companionship. Normally, pacers are allowed only in 100-mile races, but the North Face Endurance Challenge (NFEC) allows pacers for its 50-mile race. (It is worth noting, however, that the male and female runners who won the NFEC in 2013 did not use pacers at all.)

Having a companion with you during those long, late miles can make a huge difference in your race. Running long distances, often through a dark night, can leave you completely taxed; your pacer is there for safety and to help you find your way when course markings are few or your head is fuzzy.

In addition to helping navigate the course, pacers have several big jobs they can do, such as motivate, keep your pace up over a hill or when you are tiring, remind you to eat or to sip your water, calculate splits along the way, get you what you need from the aid

## What makes **a good pacer?**                                    **?**

Many and sundry qualities make for a good pacer. Much depends on the kind of runner and person that you are, what makes you tick. Consider, too, what qualities or skills you are weak on or lack, whether morale, night vision, navigational skills, or keeping track of your fueling. The right pacer can fill in those gaps. Some general qualities of a good pacer may include the following:

- A naturally enthusiastic, positive personality. Probably the most necessary characteristic of a top-notch pacer. Even when things are going well, the reassurance of an outsider's perspective can help move mountains. Likewise, the ability of your pacer to lift your spirits in time of need is dually invaluable.

- A reasonable match with your own training and skill level. This way, he or she can empathize with what you are going through and, most important, can keep up.

- Knowing you well enough to sense how you are feeling or what you need, for example, when to talk to you and when talking is too much.

Continues

Continued

- Thick-skinned and accommodating. There is no room on race day for being overly sensitive.

- Realistic and clear-headed, for example, monitoring your fueling or ensuring you are following a pace plan that will get you through stations before cutoffs.

It is beneficial to have pacers who are separate from your crew. Pacers need not only fresh legs but also fresh minds, allowing them to do some of your thinking when you are spent. If a pacer has been awake from the wee hours crewing and then has to run with you in the middle of the night, he or she may have difficulty performing at the desired level.

I was running a race once, and things weren't going well. With 20 miles to go to reach the next aid station, my mind was foggy, and I was reduced to barely shuffling, struggling along a dark country road in the middle of a moonless night. I remember at one point believing I saw a tiny baby owl just sitting on the side of the road. I asked my pacer, Scott Hajicek, "Are you seeing what I'm seeing? Scott, man, tell me, is this real?" I felt myself tipping precariously close to the edge of reason at that point in the race and so was relieved to hear Scott confirm that he, too, saw a baby owl. To be able to laugh about it together brought much-needed levity to a dark moment and a renewed faith in my ability to finish.

A good pacer can do that for you, take you out of your head when you need it, inspire you, or be there to share the challenges. So choose your pacer wisely. You want someone who knows you and with whom you feel comfortable asking for exactly what you need when you need it. You might be curt at certain moments or stressed. A good pacer won't take that to heart; it's just part of the journey.

It may also be a good strategy to shuffle in different pacers for different sections of the final miles. Maybe start with an entertaining and upbeat pacer and then shift to one who is really good at race strategy, and then finish with one who is likely to extract every bit of effort you have left in your body and mind. You need to anticipate the type of pacer you will need and match that physically and emotionally with the racecourse and your demeanor.

station, help you plot your race strategy, keep track of competitors, and pull you through tough spots where your energy and will are wilting. You'll want a pacer who takes their role seriously and who can juggle the following responsibilities:

- **Pace.** Your pacer should know what your pace needs to be to meet your goals. That way, he or she can do time calculations while on the run to help you understand how your race is unfolding. Armed with this knowledge, a pacer can answer a question such as "Can I sit down a while and still make the cutoff?" To keep you on pace, your pacer should wear a watch. A basic watch is suitable, but even better is a GPS watch, which allows the wearer to see both mileage and pace. A pacer should know the race's official cutoff time, as well as the cutoffs through each aid station, so that he or she is aware of what needs to happen and when. Typically this information can be found on the race web site or in material sent to the registered applicant. Make sure your pacer knows these times (and per-haps even carries a copy of them during the race), and both before and during the race, talk through what each cutoff means vis-à-vis your goals.

- **Motivate and encourage.** When the distance or difficulty begins to wear you down, or if you are not feeling well, a pacer is there to rally you. Whether it is telling stories to pass the time; offering words that remind, hearten, or inspire; or going out in front to give you a path to follow on a technical trail, the pacer is your chief cheerleader. Talk with your pacer beforehand about whether and how to push you in the tough moments. (This is also a good time to remind the pacer that if you say anything

### MULING

Muling is a term and a practice that comes out of the Leadville 100 and harkens back to the town's great mining past. Historically, Leadville miners used mules for hauling supplies in and out of the mountains. In much the same way, your pacer ends up being your mule—carrying your supplies, such as water bottles, extra clothes, and batteries. While muling is encouraged in Leadville, it is not allowed in most other ultras. Normally, holding something, anything, for a runner is grounds for disqualification. Be sure you and your pacers know the race rules that apply to the specific event.

sharp when he or she does try to push you, it should not be taken personally!)

- **Remind.** A pacer can remind you to eat, drink, take salt, put on sunscreen, pick up the pace, and remember the goal. The fueling reminder is particularly important. Runners commonly neglect this aspect, and proper fueling can make a race just as improper fueling can break it. Also, although pacers are there for you, do remind them in your pre-race meeting that they will need to take care of themselves, too. It is not uncommon for pacers to focus so much care on a runner that they neglect their own fueling, which can be detrimental to both of you.

- **Anticipate.** The pacer is there to think ahead for you. As you near an aid station, for example, a pacer can talk with you about what you will do there, asking questions such as "What do you want me to get you? Are you hungry? Do you need dry socks from the crew?" The pacer can then speed ahead and tell the rest of the crew how to prepare for the incoming runner.

- **Accompany.** Your pacer should be trained for the task at hand—not to the degree that you are, but I have seen struggling pacers dropped by their runners! This would most certainly be considered pacer failure. If possible, train with your pacer in the lead-up to the race. Familiarity can breed confidence and make all the difference when you are feeling fuzzy and your pacer needs to read your signals.

## Should I **go it alone?** ?

Just because pacers and crew are allowed in a race does not mean you have to use them. Although it is less common, some do go it alone.

Perhaps you desire the challenge of doing the race without support outside of what is provided by the organizer. Or perhaps you train alone and feel that adding another person into the equation would be distracting or disruptive or would put more pressure on you than you prefer. If you are very familiar with a course, a seasoned ultrarunner, or someone who knows your own highs and lows well, and you have confidence that you can inspire yourself during darker moments in the race, then going it alone is okay. Aid stations are there to meet your basic needs. And there will most likely be enough runners around you to give you the company you may want. However, remember that in smaller events, you can go for hours without seeing anyone, so in those races, a pacer is highly recommended if only for safety reasons.

And if you decide against using a pacer but then change your mind, never fear. There is usually the option of picking up a pacer during a race. Runners who are not officially part of a crew or whose runner has dropped out often hang out at aid stations. Ask a volunteer to make an announcement, and in a short time you will probably have a companion for the coming miles.

## DROP BAGS

Although aid stations will supply the basics, such as water, electrolyte drink, and a variety of snacks, they are unlikely to have all
the things you crave, prefer, and used in training. That is where
drop bags come into the ultra equation. As you prepare for race day,
think of what you need and want, and then consider what could go
askew in your race to alter your plans (such as weather, an injury,
or an unexpected eclipse). Then stock your bags accordingly. It is
also key to figure out *when* you may need various items so that you
can plant those particular bags at the appropriate station. For
example, consider when you will be running at night and be sure
you have warm clothes or extra batteries for your headlamp. If
there is a water crossing at a certain point, stock a bag with extra
shoes for the following station.

Make drop bags easy to identify so that volunteers aren't
scrambling to find them, taking precious time away from your
pace and mental focus. Drop bags also serve as backup in case
your crew miss you out on the course.
Some racecourses do not lend themselves to easy access for crewing, so
you may have to rely on a drop bag or
two before your crew can meet up
with you. And, while aid stations are
often well stocked, you never know
when they'll run out of the specific items you require at that point
in the race; your drop bag helps you prepare for that mishap. Some
races have requirements on the size of the drop bag, so check the
rules and be savvy about what you want and need.

EXPERT **TIP**

Don't forget your drop
bag when you leave
the event!

## FUELING AND HYDRATING DURING A RACE

Fueling and proper nutrition are two of the central components that set ultra distance races apart from other race distances, and they can be your biggest challenge on race day. In shorter races, you may get away with dropping the fueling ball or making some hydration mistakes. While you may not have the race you hoped for, you can usually make these errors and still handle the rigors of the race. Make those same mistakes in an ultra, however, and you greatly limit your chance of success.

As discussed in Chapter 3, what complicates this already formidable challenge is that there is no one-size-fits-all plan, as much as we might wish there were. Every athlete differs in terms of his or her specific needs, sensitivities, general health, taste, and approach. But isn't it a relief to know that there isn't only *one* route to go? Your fueling plan can be as unique as you are, and it should be! The main thing is to recognize the crucial role fueling will play in your race and never, never to leave it to chance. Don't bank on browsing at aid station buffets and still expect to perform at your best.

You need to know your body and what works for you. This comes from experimentation during your weeks and months of training for your race. This is discussed in detail in Chapters 2 and 3, so you should be heading into race day with a solid plan that has been tried and tested. Remember, what tends to be the most efficient for you is *not* necessarily the same as for your training partner or what you read in a book (yes, even this book!) but, rather, what you have tried in training and what your body is used to. You should know, intimately, your body's ease, or not, with particular electrolyte drinks or power snacks. Experimentation is what you do during your training; race day is not the time to change things up. That burrito at the aid station may look appetizing halfway through your race, but unless you've tried it in training and you've got a long and tested history of having a rock-hard stomach and digestive tract, I advise skipping it and staying on your plan. I've seen Scott Jurek down a burrito literally while running downhill during a race. My horror was exceeded only by my envy and respect. If you can do that, great. If you can't, beware. The lesson here is that you should go with what you know and what you've trained with, and leave unfamiliar treats for your post-race party.

## DINING CHEZ AID STATION

Many runners like to eat at the aid station. There you will find a variety of snacks, such as potato chips, pretzels, bananas, and M&Ms. These not only taste good, which can be a simple pleasure in the middle of an ultra, but many also have the added benefit of containing salt or sugar. While I have a food strategy that centers on gels, I'm not a complete monk at the aid station, often grabbing a handful of potato chips or a quarter of a banana if I'm feeling hungry. These are easily digested and light on the stomach and provide a refreshing change for the palate. They can serve as a treat and a bit of a motivational carrot when running from one aid station to the next.

The aid station buffets can also serve as a sort of litmus test for whether your body is running low on calories or electrolytes. If you find yourself drawn to the salty section of the station's smorgasbord (the potato chips, pretzels, salted nuts, bouillon, etc.), you may be overdoing the sweet stuff and should increase your sodium intake. And vice versa if you are drawn to the candy, fruit, and soda.

## Fluid—What, How, and When to Drink

By now it should go without saying that you should have in your bottle what you've tested out in training. The powered drink mixes are especially nice on race day because you can customize for taste and calories, adding more or less, depending on how strong you prefer the taste to be. I know a number of runners who will make their own hydration compositions, mixing together more than one brand. That said, tracking your calorie intake is harder when you customize, so do the math and keep a close eye on how much you are consuming.

Take along the flavor (or flavors) you like, customizing to your taste, because in the end, you don't want to have something in your bottle that you don't want to drink. I tend to tire of sweet electrolyte drinks after a while, and so rather than drinking less, I carry two bottles, one with ice water and one with electrolyte. The water refreshes me in a way that the electrolyte drink cannot. However, bear in mind that if you choose to go with water only in your bottles, you will need to take care of calories and salts in other ways.

There are various philosophies on hydration strategies. One elite runner I know will drink only water for the first half of the race, and then only electrolyte drink for the second half. His theory is that he gets a stronger boost from the calories and salts in the second half, just when he really needs it. Another runner I know takes this a step further, searching for a stronger hit from the electrolyte by going the first 2 hours of the race without drinking at all, and

EXPERT **TIP**

I run with bottles because that is what I prefer; however, a hydration backpack will allow you to carry far more liquid: up to two liters!

then drinking an electrolyte. I think this is a risky idea, due to the catastrophic effects that can result from even mild dehydration.

Don't play games that might allow your hydration to slip away from you. In any ultra, but in particular the warmer ones, you are always riding a thin line between being hydrated and not, and the price you pay as you slip into dehydration is high: loss of appetite, less saliva produced, food not digesting as easily, cramping, and many other deleterious effects.

In a race in milder conditions, I will drink 16 ounces per hour. The more extreme the temperatures, the more I endeavor to stay on top of my drink and up the ounces per hour. In the 2013 Western States, for example, in temperatures of 80 to 90 degrees, I started the race carrying two 13-ounce bottles, tucked behind my back. The belt I used carries one bottle nicely, but a second bottle was one too many, and I experienced some unfortunate chafing from it. Still, I knew I needed those extra ounces to stay hydrated between stations. Soon, even that wasn't enough. I was consistently out of water well before each aid station. After 25 miles, I picked up a 24-ounce bottle as a handheld, which means that for the remainder of the race, I was drinking nearly 40 ounces per hour.

**EXPERT TIP**

Avoid fueling on uphills, unless you are walking. Drink on level ground or on downhills when your heart rate isn't as high. Take care fueling on technical descents.

A lot of people don't like carrying all that liquid, complaining that it weighs them down. My advice to them is pretty simple: If you don't like carrying that extra weight, drink it. You get the liquid you need, and you also get a lighter bottle—win-win. *Do not* squirt it out! That's a bad idea, believe me.

I once ran a race in which I was fatigued and irritated by the heaviness of the bottles I was carrying. I dumped some water out of the bottles soon after leaving an aid station, only to find myself facing 7 miles with 2,000 feet of elevation gain before the next aid station on a hot day. I ended up desperately wishing for that water

**EXPERT TIP**

Drink in the aid station as you get the bottle filled. That way, you leave the station hydrated and still have plenty in your bottles or pack for the road ahead.

back as I sucked at a dry, empty bottle. Some races, like Western States or the Vermont 100, have a lot of aid stations; most do not, however, or the aid stations might be separated by significant summits, as in Leadville. The fluid in your bottles or pack may be all that you get for many hours during maximum exertion. Fill 'er up and deal with the weight.

## MONITORING WEIGHT LOSS DURING A RACE

A common way to monitor an athlete's health during a race is via the scale. Most 100-milers have aid stations with medical representation (some 100Ks and 50-milers do as well). At these checkpoints, volunteers will get you on the scale and compare your current weight against your starting weight.

This is a way of gauging possible dehydration or, conversely, water retention, which can be a sign of a dangerous condition called hyponatremia. It is also a way for experienced personnel to assess each runner's mental clarity during a strategic point in the race. At the Pine to Palm 100, we begin to profile runners at mile 26 and do so again at 65 miles and then again at the finish. Some races weigh runners more and some less, but know that it is for your safety as well as for the volunteers and other runners who may become compromised if something happens during the event.

The weight-loss rule of thumb is this: If the scale shows you have lost 3 percent of your weight, you will be warned to make an active effort to get on top of your hydration. If you have lost 5 percent, you might be told to sit a while in the tent and drink. If you have lost 7 percent, generally you will not be allowed to leave the aid station at all, or you may have to demonstrate active rehydration, such as drinking two bottles of fluid and eating a bowl of soup, as a way of getting you back on track. But, frankly, for many runners, reaching the 7 percent loss mark means their race is over.

Conversely, if the scale shows that you have gained weight, this might be a sign of hyponatremia, in which you are not processing fluids because your kidneys and stomach are shutting down. Hyponatremia is not as common as dehydration and is harder to gauge, since runners often will come into a station heavier because they are wet or are wearing more or different clothing.

Remember, though, weight can be a tricky gauge of health during a race. For example, I tend to weigh the same amount throughout my training: 168 pounds. As I taper over the last week or two, my weight typically goes up thanks to the added calories in/fewer calories out and the extra water I'm consuming to keep my hydration topped off days before the race. When I'm weighed at the expo, the number can be misleading because a lot of the weight, in particular the water, is going to drop off during the race, making it difficult to tell if that loss is problematic and is signaling a true health problem. A far better gauge of health is when medical staff or volunteers look at you, talk with you, assess if you are coherent, and generally get a sense of how you're feeling, in addition to weighing you.

## PACE ON RACE DAY

Setting a pace on race day involves something of a balancing act. When you first set off from the start line, you are bound to be contending with wayward nerves, unharnessed adrenaline, and race-pace envy. Be aware that all of this is affecting you, and try your best to patiently let the race unfold. You have time, plenty of it, to figure out what move to make and when. Don't get panicky or excited in the early miles, feeding off of the high-flying anxiety all around you.

Steel yourself to let things fall into place in the first 5 miles, or about an hour, as you run on pure adrenaline. After that time, most runners settle down into their most comfortable pace. You, too, will fall into a comfortable rhythm with the folks around you as your pace settles in. So don't burn a lot of energy in the first hour or so fretting over where you should be in the pack. Be patient; things will get sorted out, with relatively little time lost. In those first miles, you really aren't running your own race yet. It can be hard in the early miles to strike out at your own pace, particularly if a trail is singletrack and single file.

That said, is there ever a reason to go out faster than you've trained? Maybe. Sometimes the combination of cooler air and fresh legs makes for great running conditions. If you are in a climate that is going to get hot later in the day, then you may want to consider speeding up your pace to get miles out of the way early, while it's still cool. The same is true if you are trying to get in some extra daylight miles, racing against the coming darkness.

# TOP 10 **MUST DO'S** ON RACE DAY

||||||||||||||||||||||||||||||||||||||||||||||||||||||||||||||||||||||||||||||||||||||||||||||||||

**1** **DO be patient.** The race ahead is long; allow it to unfold, and remind yourself to appreciate and enjoy the journey.

**2** **DO be gentle on yourself beforehand.** Take it easy the day and night prior to race day. Race organizers don't make that easy, by scheduling interesting expos and panel discussions the day before, where you are on your feet, walking around, expending energy. Discipline yourself to keep that to a minimum, making a conscious effort to sit and rest, with your feet up as much as possible. Don't squander the good work you've done during your taper in the last day or two.

**3** **DO wear a watch.** I rely on my watch not only to know if I am on race pace but also for proper and strategic eating and hydrating. For example, I know I want to eat a gel every 20 to 30 minutes; I know I want to drink an entire bottle of fluid in an hour. A watch keeps me on that plan. Some people rely on aid station placement to some degree. However, that involves an intimate knowledge of the course that most runners don't have, and it also allows the aid station to dictate your fueling pace, which should be in your control. Your watch is the fail-safe. Wear it.

**4** **DO fuel often and early.** Attempting to play catch-up later in the race is a dangerous and mostly doomed proposition. For one, you process sugar and food poorly near the end of a race. Also, as you tire, it is easy to forget to fuel properly later in a race. Don't get to the point of being either hungry or thirsty. Load on the front end.

**5** **DO have more than one goal.** That way, if your primary goal goes out the window, you can reach for your secondary or tertiary goal. For example, a top goal may be going for first place in your age group. A secondary goal could be more time-focused, such as going for a sub-24-hour race in a 100-miler. A tertiary goal might be simply to finish.

**6** **DO be ready to be resilient when things go wrong.** If you roll an ankle or your breathing is erratic or your stomach goes, you and your crew will have to think on the fly. Be ready for and open to that. If you have severe cramping, for example, a plan-on-the-fly might be: We will walk through this rather than just sitting down and doing nothing. Or, I will run for 2 minutes and walk 2 minutes. Mentally, devising a plan gives you back and keeps you in control. Micromanage the problem while still keeping an eye on the big picture.

**7 DO push yourself a little.** This is a race, after all. And you've trained hard for this day, maybe years of cumulative effort, maybe 6 months straight of prioritizing training over other things in your life. You deserve to claim all that you've worked for. So go for it! Don't be tentative. Push yourself up some of those hills, find that pace that you've trained for, and stick with it. Don't be afraid to set your sights a little bit higher on the dream you've worked toward—embrace it!

**8 DO visualize success.** During every race, I see myself winning. Whatever it may be, you must have something that inspires you held like a beacon in your mind—maybe it is winning the race or your age group, or maybe it is the act of crossing the finish line. Visualize success. Visualize the course. Visualize getting through specific aid stations. As for me, in tough moments in a race, I see a reenactment of some of my best finish line scenarios all melded into one.

**9 DO have fun.** Make the most of the day, and be grateful for the unique opportunity to be there. When things go awry, remind yourself that you are there for fun, and enjoy the day you've been given as it unfolds. Be present.

**10 DO stay aware.** Most races are run in the wilds. The course will not be entirely flagged nor each turn highlighted. Pay attention to where you are, be familiar with the course beforehand, and know the markings. If you can get on the course for some reconnaissance before race day, do it. If not, online maps make examining the course easy. Have basic knowledge of where you are going, and know the names of the trails you will be on and where the ascents and descents will be. Do not just mentally check out when you are running; it is your responsibility to stay on the course. Knowing details about it will help you gain confidence when it begins to seem like it's been too long since you've spotted that last race marker.

# TOP 10 **DO NOTS** ON RACE DAY

**1** **DO NOT try something new on race day.** I recall a friend who was preparing for a race and asked to borrow a hydration pack. I brought her one the night before the race, one designed to also hold bottles on the front of pack. She'd never tried something like it before and found it awkward. However, without another option, she had no choice but to use it. The most important race of the year for her, one she had been working toward for months, and she was about to use something she'd never used before. In the end, the worst physical problem that resulted was chafing. But her anxiety level, due to using something she'd never tried before, was high. Don't open yourself up to failure by experimenting with something new on race day. That is what practice is for. Go with what gives you confidence, so that you can trust in the products you're using. Don't rely on luck. And don't sabotage yourself.

**2** **DO NOT go out too hard.** Race excitement and adrenaline combined with the week's prior taper and resting might lull you into going out harder than you planned; after all, you feel fresh and strong! You might be able to get away with going out too hard in a half-marathon or marathon, but in an ultra race, the price you pay for that is high. Remember this: If you feel you are going out too slow, slow down. Pay attention to your watch, pay attention to your training, keep tabs on a comparable runner, whatever it takes.

**3** **DO NOT leave loose ends as far as the responsibilities of your pacers, crew, and family members.** Do your due diligence prior to race morning so that you are not trying to communicate new information at the last minute, amid everything else that is going on. Make sure people know where they need to go, what they need to do, what they should have for you, and that they should be prepared to be nimble if things go wrong. Also know the apropos logistical details, such as how many people you can have at an aid station. Finding out this information late can change your plans, something that can cause unnecessary last-minute panic. Due diligence also applies to knowing the course in advance so that your crew can help you. If there is a huge descent in the dark at mile 70, you need to know that and be sure your crew are equipped with headlamps for you and for them. Or if you know that at mile 80 it will be cold, make sure your crew have a jacket and a hat for you. At that point in a race, you might not be churning out much heat—you will want that coverage. Be prepared.

 **DO NOT panic!** Nothing good ever comes from panic. Things may go wrong or not as planned; you might not feel good, you might not know where you are on the course. Just regroup—do not unravel. Take solace in knowing that an ultra is a long way, and the beauty of that is that problems often work themselves out over the long haul. Stomach problems can subside; things can completely turn around. Have patience, and don't panic.

**DO NOT fret over natural phenomena.** Western States 2013 was run in crazy record heat. You have no control over temperature. Or maybe your racecourse changes the week before due to a flood or a fire. These decisions are out of your hands. You can only perform for what you've prepared for and what is in your control. Rely on all the other strong points of your training. True preparation means preparing for the unknown. If you know there is, historically, a good chance of rain during your race, be ready with the gear. (Be ready, too, to combat the chafing that may come with that.) I once ran Leadville, and at 12,000 feet on Hope Pass, it started to snow. I had no gloves, so I ran with my hands down my pants for several miles. Let's not even talk about how this affected my running form and fatigued me unnecessarily. Do your best to prepare for surprises from Mother Nature, but don't let them throw you off your game. Weather happens, and it helps to remember that everyone in the race will face the same conditions; there is something reassuring in knowing that you aren't going it alone. Plan for adversity as best you can, and let the rest go.

 **DO NOT lose track of time.** It's easy to do while you chat with other runners on the course. Similarly, don't stop paying attention to where you are. Cutoffs in ultra races always loom—so know how far you have to be and when so that you can make your end goal.

**7** **DO NOT squander time at aid stations.** Have a plan for what you want to accomplish at the station, and stick to it. Western States has 20 aid stations; just 2 extra minutes at each station can set you back 40 minutes. Yes, aid stations are a refuge and a respite. But, remember, they are there simply to provide nutrition and some maintenance to get you out and on your way. Refuel, yes. Fill water, yes. But keep moving.

Some folks stop, indecisive about what to eat. Know what you want and need before you get there. Then get your potato chips and go. And remember, aid station workers often will respond in kind: If you seem unhurried, they may feel free to chat and take things slowly. Send a message that you are there to fuel and go. Have the lids off of your water bottles by the time you walk into the station, which shows that you mean business. Often runners want to adjust laces, remove sand, put on sunscreen, and that is fine, but just know that when you sit down, it will feel extremely comfortable, and you may not feel that extra 5 or 10 minutes passing.

Be hypersensitive to time. If I am in a good rhythm, I might not stop at all, depending on how close the next station is. You certainly need enough calories and water to last; don't skimp. But avoid the allure of the aid station, the music and food, the seduction of everyone hanging out. Remind yourself that your goal is to get to the finish as quickly as you can; *then* you can party.

**8** **DO NOT be rude to volunteers.** Thank them for being there and show your appreciation. Acknowledge them. I have seen some appalling rudeness at stations, such as a runner yelling at a volunteer to get out of a chair because he wanted to sit down, or another runner yelling because she had to wait a few moments for the soup pot to be refilled. This is totally unacceptable. Those helping out at aid stations are people, volunteering their personal time for you. Treat them with the respect they deserve.

**9** **DO NOT let aid stations dictate your personal fueling, waiting to eat or drink until you arrive there and eating whatever happens to be at that station.** Customize how you eat and drink to suit your highly personal habits, preferences, and training, using handheld bottles or hydration packs, carrying gels if you use those, or whole foods if that is what you prefer. Whatever it is, have it planned out, and take it with you. Fuel often and early, and stick to your own personalized schedule.

**10** **DO NOT lose sight of your humanity.** If a runner rolls an ankle, take the time to offer your help. If someone is struggling, ask if he or she needs water or salt or if there is anything you can do. If someone is in distress, don't forget that this is a hobby. Do not become numb to your fellow racers. Once, during a 50-mile race, I came upon a competitor who, at 25K, had fallen and possibly broken a bone. I was with a friend, who stayed with him, and I ran ahead to the aid station to alert them. During Western States 2013, I saw one of my top competitors, Cameron Clayton, take the wrong road. Letting him make that mistake would certainly be no way to win. We all yelled to get him back on course. There are certain graces that must always be maintained, in racing as in life, even among your toughest competitors.

## CUTOFF TIMES

Cutoffs are set times by which you must reach each aid station or be disqualified. These times are listed in the event information packet, and you should be familiar with them and how they stack up against your planned pace.

Some runners never experience the stress of struggling to make cutoff times. Front- and mid-packers don't typically bump up against these times, although anything can happen across many miles—such as getting lost or spending time caring for a bad blister or other physical complication—that pushes you toward a cutoff. Slower runners who are dialed in to their pace are able to approximate the time they need to reach certain points on the course and should coordinate with their pacers and crew to keep them on task. By doing so, they often avoid cutting it close. Some runners, however, spend the race fighting to get to aid stations before the set cutoff time. This can create a very stressful race and an obviously unpleasant experience.

As race director of Pine to Palm, I've gotten angry e-mails from frustrated runners who had arrived at an aid station feeling in decent shape to go on but were deeply disappointed to find they did not make the cutoff and had to end their race. To have come that far and not be allowed to complete the race seemed to them very unfair. I certainly understand that disappointment. But cutoffs are not set to be unfair; quite the opposite. If cutoff times were fuzzy or judged on a case-by-case basis, inevitably they would be unfair to someone. A race is manned for only so many hours, and volunteers are committed for a designated period. Thus, cutoffs need to be fixed and inflexible. If you miss a cutoff, avoid getting angry or upset with the volunteers who are managing the station. Asking aid station captains to let you go on is not right. It is not their decision, so don't put them in that awkward position.

If you find yourself in a situation where your race comes to an early end due to not making the cutoff time, remind yourself to be proud of whatever mileage you ran. And restrategizing for the next time can be a fun and powerful motivator. I remember my dad missed a Boston qualifying time by 18 seconds one year and 19 seconds the next. Frustrating? You bet. But he would be the first to tell you that it made qualifying, which he did the third time around, that much sweeter.

## MENTAL FOCUS ON RACE DAY—TIPS AND STRATEGIES

An ultra race is mental as much as it is physical, maybe more so. You certainly should pull from the confidence you have in what you've done physically to prepare, but don't underestimate the mental piece. Ultra distances can be intimidating, and despite logging solid, strong miles in training, chances are you have not done this distance on this course. Don't let that throw you off; remind yourself that you've done the distance in smaller chunks. For example, when you cross the 50-mile mark in a 100-miler, remind yourself that you've already done that distance and can do it one more time, or tell yourself as you pass the halfway point in a 50-miler that there is really just a marathon to go. These little tricks are great perspective changers when the distance threatens to overwhelm.

Like most runners, you've probably already developed a few of your own mental tricks without really knowing you were doing it. Pay attention to what motivates you and what doesn't, and if different things work on different types of days. And if you need a few new ones to add to your repertoire, here are some more mental tricks to try:

- Break up the immense task at hand by setting smaller objectives along the way, such as getting from one aid station to another or one landmark to another, or reaching certain elevations on a big climb. Each smaller goal reached gets you that much closer to the big goal.
- Visualize getting through certain familiar mile markers (e.g., 50K, 26.2 miles, 10K), running each as a mini-race. When I ran the John Muir Trail in 2013, I had never done many of those

stretches before, so I would visualize stretches of an equal distance that I had done in the past. This method helped remind me that I had the strength and experience I needed, which gave me confidence.

- Positive self-talk goes a long way. I often encourage myself in the third person, a voice from that reassuring inner cheerleader: *You've done the training, Hal. You are ready for this. You got this!*

- Take your mind off a churning stomach, sore legs, worries, or long miles with mantras or chants that you repeat over and over, or try counting to 100 or counting backward.

- Think back on other successes, recalling past struggles through which you endured and, ultimately, prevailed. Remind yourself that you know how to get through rough patches and that it is worth it, that you'll soon feel better, just as you have with other races or other challenges in life.

- Talk with fellow runners and tap into the excitement of the race to pull you through difficult periods.

- Get competitive. Go after the next runner in your sights and then the next, racing along even if you aren't near the front of the pack.

- Focus on your strengths. If you are a strong climber, use the ascent as a time to refuel your confidence, passing other racers and encouraging them to share some positive energy. Hopefully, they will return the favor if they catch you up on the flats or the descents.

- Tap into the physical beauty that surrounds you. Kilian Jornet fuels himself from the views, the plant life, the mountains. Chanel your inner Kilian, dancing the trails, frolicking in nature.

- Remind yourself that you chose to be there. You paid for this. You committed to it. You are going to get it done.

- Won't your family and friends be proud of you for such an accomplishment? Will you inspire your coworkers to lead more healthy lifestyles? Will your discipline in training for and then completing this ultra help motivate those you care about to do what they do with a similar drive, pursuing their passion to achieve their goals?
- Yiannis Kouros, a Greek ultrarunner who holds almost every record for races longer than 100 miles, uses poetry, music, and other art to inspire him to perform at his highest level. But if you listen to music, do so at a level quiet enough that you can hear other runners approaching, or put the headphone in only one ear so you will be safe out on the trail.

## TALKING ON THE RUN

Back when I started running, it was nearly always by myself; looking back at it now, I see my training as, well, rather monkish. Not because I sought out alone time but because I didn't have many peers at that time who wanted to go out and run for hours on end. So when I got to an event, after training alone for months, I relished chatting with peers and being able to share the trail or road with people with whom I had something so deep and intrinsic in common. Besides being a great outlet for me, I found that this socializing had a practical effect: It took the edge off the nervousness I felt at an event's start. All the fun and chatter eased early morning jitters and kept me from getting caught up in the enormity of the task ahead and the gaping chasm between me and the finish line. Another practical effect is that, while talking can feel fatiguing later in a race, early on it helps conserve energy and keep you on pace. If you find that you can talk comfortably as you run, then you have not gone out too fast, a common error.

That said, there is a time when my enthusiasm for chat wears off and I turn all of my concentration and focus to the task at hand. This point is different for everyone. For me, I find that I can talk comfortably for about 10 percent of the time. Others I know are able to be social for an entire event, something I can't fathom. Just remember, socializing during a race has its own rules of etiquette. As the race goes on, people around you are going through highs and lows, getting worn out. Speaking while trying to put out a solid effort can be difficult. It is common for a runner to want to retreat into his or her inner space at some points in the journey. Be sensitive to that and resist being overly talkative at times or expecting the multisyllabic responses that are part of a normal conversation. If you are the tired one, don't feel obligated to talk, as you might in a regular social environment. At times, I have simply apologized and confessed that it is all I can do just to focus on finishing. Don't be afraid to speak up. I've never met an ultra runner who didn't understand.

## RACING WITH FRIENDS

For some, running is a solo hobby, a time for reflection and solitude. For others, it is all about running together and sharing the experience. Some may train alone out of necessity and look to races as an opportunity to share their passion with other ultrarunners. As discussed in Chapter 2, running with a friend or group during training can be fun and motivating. However, running together in a race requires more planning and coordination. Certainly, it offers some great benefits. It is a great feeling to work together and motivate each other and also to have a companion to share the highs and lows across the many miles. At some point, though, you may want to push yourself beyond that. Have a plan if something goes

## NASAL STRIPS

I often get asked about the strip I usually wear across my nose during races. The bandage's aim is to widen the nasal cavity, making breathing easier, which for me has proven to be very useful. The ability to breathe through my nose is key on a few levels. One, the strip opens up my nasal passages, which sometimes close on me, thanks to bad sinuses and allergic sensitivities. That widening makes me more comfortable. Two, wearing the strip helps me to take in as much oxygen as possible and to breathe with control. When those pathways are restricted, I can't mange the relaxed breathing that I crave; instead, my breathing becomes labored and quick. When I am able to breathe through my nose, I feel calm. I even use this as a gauge: If I can't breathe through my nose, it means I am going too fast.

wrong or if someone slows. Will you stay together? Or will you stay on goal pace and leave others behind? To avoid misunderstandings, consider talking about your plans and goals beforehand, so that mutual expectations are set.

I've raced alongside a runner for tens of miles, as we pushed one another in the best ways, and then broke away in the last miles, making the move to win. I've had others leave me, too. It is a race, after all, and it's yours to run. But I've also deliberately shared a finish, and, perhaps surprisingly, that memory is one of my favorites.

The event was a 50-miler in Arizona, the Crown King Scramble. Due to the heat, the race started at an ungodly 2:00 a.m., and to make things tougher, there had been a massive thunderstorm only hours earlier, with flash flooding that left the largely uphill course a sea of mud. A fellow competitor and I slogged through 30 miles of this, uphill and side by side, with enormous globs of mud stuck to our feet. It was exhausting and an ankle break waiting to happen. We worked together to get through it, however, realizing we were battling this course far more than each other. We powered through, then hit the final climb. After the climb, the course ran 2 miles steeply downhill into the mining town where the finish lay. I knew if I was going to break away, now was the time to do it. Beaten down by the course and the elements, we looked at one other and asked, "So are we going to race this thing?" We decided to run it in together, instead, and share a victory that was so hard fought. After 47 miles, with only a few miles to go, we figured we had suffered together and would finish together. We beat the course!

This story illustrates a facet I find unique to ultrarunning: that you can be very competitive or not competitive at all. Unlike in some other sports, the thing that gets you through an endurance event may not be the podium or a first-place medal. Sometimes it is beating your best friend or a mentor you've looked up to forever. Sometimes it is simply sharing the journey. The key is finding the thing that drives you in that race, whatever it may be; this will arm you with the staying power to make it through to the finish.

## PASSING ON SINGLETRACK

When folks picture trail running, they most often imagine single-track. Unlike fire roads or double-wide hiking trails, singletracks are the narrow dirt paths, usually smooth and flowing, that are often the subject of beautiful photos depicting dream trail runs.

Both nimble footing and etiquette come into play when racing on singletrack. Avoid crowding someone unnecessarily. During

Western States one year, we started in a pack, with everyone falling into his or her own space within the first mile or so, as is often the case. However, I remember one runner remained right at my back, not backing off but not passing either; a few times I felt him clip my heels. I felt boxed in, and we still had 95 miles to go. Irritated, I wanted to tell him that I found his spacing claustrophobic, but not wanting to be rude, I instead mumbled something along the lines of, "Hey, we're going to be together all day, so..." He didn't get my subtle message. I eventually pulled away, but the burst of energy required to do so pushed me harder than I cared to go at that point in the race. In retrospect, I should have spoken plainly.

So if you come upon another runner, don't ride his or her back. Either leave space between you or make it plain you want to pass, announcing yourself as you would on a bike: "I'm on your left." The runner should step aside if there is enough room or when the trail widens. By the way, headphones can make hearing other runners difficult, so you may need to touch someone on the shoulder lightly to let them know you want to pass.

## DNF: WHEN IS ENOUGH ENOUGH?

In my very first 100-miler, I rolled an ankle as I crossed a cow pasture 7 miles into the race. I had come into the race still healing from a slight ankle injury when I stumbled upon that hole in the dirt and badly rolled the ankle. It hurt, and I knew I'd done damage, but there was no way I was stopping 7 miles into a race that I had put so much heart, hope, and time into.

Fast-forward to mile 80, where it had turned into a contusion, with not only my ankle but also my shin hugely swollen. With a painful, Frankenstein-style limp, I dragged myself and that ankle for 20 more miles. I'm not sure how I managed to continue through the pain, except to say that I was in the lead and running on pure adrenaline. I remember telling myself I absolutely had to keep going, that I owed it to myself to get it done. But time moved at a painful crawl, and instead of those last miles taking me 3 or 4 hours, they took triple that. Furthermore, that ankle has plagued me my entire career. Looking back, it wasn't a smart decision to finish that race.

On the flip side, I recall racing the Leadville 100 in 2010. I find it easy to remember the year because the race was the week before my wedding. You may wonder why I was racing a 100-miler just days before my wedding? It is a valid question. For one, I had finished a 100-miler every year since my first one in 1999, and I didn't want to break my 11-year streak. Not only that, but I had been a champion of the Western States 100, and to also win the Leadville 100 is something that no athlete had yet done and so was a driving force behind my desire to do the race. So I made a deal with my wife. We agreed that I could do it as long as I promised not to screw up my body before the wedding.

Although I'd run it before, the 2010 race turned out to be one of the toughest I've ever run. I trace the problem to getting lost twice, and as a way of trying to get back into the race as a contender, I foolishly ran like a madman over Hope Pass (elevation 12,600 feet). Feeling completely spent and unstable and shaky from running so hard at altitude, I began vomiting.

I recall phoning my soon-to-be wife at a desperate point in the race, teetering on the verge of dehydration and not entirely coherent, telling her that I wanted to quit, to which she replied, "Why don't you just walk?" Walk? With a goal of winning this double victory on my mind, no way was I going to walk the rest of the way. But without another viable option, I did walk from Treeline to Fish Hatchery, less than 10 miles, from mile 70 to mile 80, for 2 long hours. And then I quit. Yes, quit.

I regret that decision. Not because I don't think it is OK to quit; sometimes it is. I regret it because I know now that dropping that day was due to an error in mental preparation, something within my control. Could I have walked to the finish line? Probably, yes. But my goal was winning, and so I had only imagined myself flying through Fish Hatchery on my way to crowning glory. Hobbling at a walking pace for another 20 miles was not part of my plan, psychologically, and threatened to take a physical toll I did not want to pay. The main thing was, I was mentally beaten down, had no B goal, and so was completely unprepared for this turn of events.

What I needed that day was to have more than one goal for the race. If one of my goals had been to finish, I could have walked to the end and met that goal, turning that race into the success it deserved to be instead of a failure I don't like to recall.

These stories recount different experiences with quite different end results. They illustrate two major points of consideration in figuring out when enough is enough. One, establish A, B, and C goals before your race and share these with your supporters, crew, and pacers. With tiered goals and team backup, you are more likely to achieve success. Two, if you start to get into problems that are going to hurt you, call it.

Sometimes after an event, we suffer from subtle amnesia—you forget about the pain and the problems, and as you stand around after the fact, clearheaded, you kick yourself, thinking, *I could have/should have.* But remind yourself that, in the moment, you

## TIPS FOR **HOW AND WHEN TO MAKE THE CALL**

- Check the clock. Given your pace and the time on the clock, will you have time to finish within the race's prescribed time frame and make the cutoffs?

- Take input from your team. They can't always turn things around, but sometimes they can. They can't always stop you from going on, but sometimes they can. Encourage your crew to nudge you when exhaustion and aches cloud your judgment, but also let your crew know that pain and suffering have a finite ending that commands respect. There will be other races.

- If possible, dip into prior experience to help make a decision. Know your own fortitude and limits.

- Ask yourself, "What am I willing to go through for this event?" Know the answer going in.

- Review your goals for the race. Are any still attainable?

- Push away the demons. You knew there would be pain; try making friends with it, not giving in to it.

- Some things work themselves out with time: bad stomach, fatigue, aches, nausea, getting lost. Give yourself the time to get things in check before making a decision to drop.

- Some things do *not* work themselves out: badly rolled ankles, broken bones, serious cuts, bleeding. If you get very dehydrated or hypothermic, for example, it is difficult if not impossible to turn that around in a race. Drop before you do further damage.

made the choices that you needed to make at that time, having tapped yourself completely. Or you wisely prepared your support team, and they helped you make the tough decision.

## COOLING DOWN AFTER THE RACE

Cooling down following an ultra is a different animal altogether than after a faster-paced race such as a 10K or half-marathon. In those races, your body is usually going at a pace from which stopping abruptly is ill-advised. In an ultra, in contrast, your body has typically been maintaining a fairly easy, steady pace for a long time. So as you cross that coveted finish line, your body is not likely at the height of exertion. Still, a brief cooldown is appropriate. While you may wish to drop to the ground as soon as the finish line is behind you, this is not the best idea. You've certainly earned the right to relax, but lying down or sitting can make you lose blood pressure or even faint, from both exhaustion and dehydration. So walk round a bit before you sit.

You may be surprised at how chilled you feel after a race—body shaking, teeth chattering, even on a warm day. Be prepared by having warm, fresh, dry clothing at the finish; I will often add two new layers soon after I've finished a race. A down puffy works remarkably well for helping you to regulate your core temperature at the finish. And come prepared with footwear—flip-flops, sandals, or clogs. Believe me, you will want to take off your shoes, so have something to put on that allows for expansion of your feet and possible bloody toenails or blisters.

Continue to take in those fluids. Comforting, warm soup is often available at the end of a race. Hot coffee also works well because the caffeine helps you maintain your blood pressure and prevents fainting or dizziness.

Once you do sit, keep your feet up as much as you can. Get the recovery process started as soon as possible by drinking or eating a post-race recovery protein, as well as some additional carbs. You will soon sleep, but remember, that's another 8 hours of not recovering, making your body wait for the nutrition it needs to effectively bounce back. I will drink a protein shake or a fruit smoothie with added protein—both are easily digested. If you prefer, you can try a bit of solid food, and if it sits well, after a few minutes, eat some more. Just about anything you consume will be utilized by your depleted body. This will both help you warm up and lift your energy and spirits after the flood of adrenaline has left your body once you've crossed the finish line.

Remember that after you do sit, standing back up is going to be hard. Taking a warm shower as soon as you are able does wonders for both cleaning you up and warming you up, body and soul.

Compression clothing, especially if you have a long flight or car ride ahead before you get any post-race sleep, is also helpful. Ultra-runners may have a higher susceptibility to blood clots, which can occur when long periods of inactivity follow strenuous activity. Periodic movement, elevated legs, and compression gear are appropriate precautions.

# 8
# TRAINING
# **PLANS**

JUST LIKE YOU, I LOVE TO RUN. WHEN I BEGAN TO LOG
mileage daily and monthly, I was quite conservative and strict with
the guidelines I set for myself. I credit this prudent time and solid
foundation with helping me avoid serious injury and overuse issues
when I went to the well, time after time, later in my career. I found
that the key to preserving my body as well as my energy and drive
was to progress slowly. My running life started with a 3-mile daily
route that I repeated earnestly for many months before stepping up
in distance. Once I had the confidence and tolerance, I shed my jean

shorts and all their comforts for the move up to proper running shorts, and a 7-mile and eventual 10-mile regimen. (Seriously, jean shorts.) This didn't happen overnight; I took a year or more to find my stride, just like some of you may have done or are doing. I encourage you to build that all-important solid base for the rigors of these training plans.

For a beginner, it sometimes seems as if there can never be too much of a good thing. Motivation and excitement mix and become a seductive elixir from which big gains evolve. I would caution you to take it slowly, however. Doing so helps you to avoid injury, over-training, and burnout. Now, I know that the ultra distance attracts a certain personality to its door, and there are plenty of runs in here to take advantage of that zeal, but please heed the progressions in these plans if you are new to the distance. I promise it will help you keep on enjoying ultras for a long time.

## INTENSITY WORKOUTS

These next pages provide detailed plans to help you achieve ultra success. The mileage is easy enough to follow, but sometimes that isn't enough to maintain a progressive build. Training is more than just putting in more and more miles, although that is certainly key. There also needs to be some intensity built into your training program. I am a firm believer that intense workouts must be separated by at least 10 to 12 days to allow for recovery and proper performance when called upon. With that in mind, I have suggested days on which to add one of the intensity workouts to your daily mileage. You will notice that these workouts generally follow a 2-week cycle, to allow for other moderate training exercises that will exist within the plan and bring diversity.

### Tempo Runs

Tempo runs are inserted during peak training weeks to enhance the feel of a race day effort and to make your body more efficient for the duration of the event. (For more detail on tempo runs, see page 29.) The key is to work on your rhythm and tempo for an hour at a comfortably hard pace.

### Fartleks

Fartleks ("speed play") are designed to provide some change of pace for the legs, since most of the running at this time is at an easy pace. For fartlek training, run a 1-minute surge every 6 or 7 minutes for the entirety of the run. This surge is not terribly hard, perhaps 15 to 20 seconds per mile faster than your normal long-run pace. At the end of the surge, simply return to your relaxed rhythm. If you are having a hard time returning to your normal long-run pace, lower the speed of your surges.

### Hill Repeats

Hill repeats are another tool for building strength, and they also give you greater confidence come race day. Locate a consistent grade on which to perform your repeats. The key is to do a sustainable effort for 90 seconds followed by a 2- to 3-minute cooldown, and to repeat this 10 times. Ideally, you would work this exercise into the designated run, perhaps running to your preferred stretch of climb as a warm-up and back again for the cooldown. (For more detail on hill work, see pages 27–28.)

## TRAINING RACES

Although the training plans do not specifically schedule preparatory training races, I urge you to factor these in. Putting yourself in race situations is a smart, useful, and confidence-building strategy. I was never one to turn down a race. I remember a spring season leading up to Western States where I raced a 50K, a 50-miler, and a 100K on successive weekends. This was probably overkill, but pushing myself against competition was something I wasn't able to replicate with ease in my day-to-day training. I found the pull of a race very motivating, and it helped to harden my legs for the big day. It also gave me leeway to make mistakes off the main stage and with less serious consequences. These are all great reasons for you to supplement some of your scheduled long runs with events. I would not recommend racing an ultra in advance of a 50-miler or 100-miler any earlier than 4 weeks out from the day of your race. You will need to adapt your schedule to accommodate a slight taper going in and recovery coming out of these races.

## THE PLANS—50K, 50 MILES TO 100K, AND 100 MILES

The plans in this book are laid out to be progressive, with a healthy and exciting buildup of both mileage and appropriate intensity. You'll find the weekly mileage to be straightforward and easy to follow. There are also targeted workouts in the plans, built in alongside your miles, which will build your strength and also give you opportunities to customize the amplitude of your workouts.

## ULTRA TRAINING PLAN—50K

| WEEK | MON | TUES | WED | THURS | FRI | SAT | SUN | TOTAL |
|---|---|---|---|---|---|---|---|---|
| 1 | 6 | 6 | 4 (a.m.) / 4 (p.m.) | 6 | 4 | 13 | 7 | 50 |
| 2 | off | 6 | 8 | 4 (a.m.) / 4 (p.m.) | 4 | 15 | 9 | 50 |
| 3 | off | 8 | 5 (a.m.) / 5 (p.m.) | 6 | 6 | 18 | 9 | 57 |
| 4 | off | 8 | 8 | 8 | 8 | 15 | 11 | 58 |
| 5 | off | 8 | 8 | 5 (a.m.) / 5 (p.m.) | 8 | 13 | 13 | 60 |
| 6 | off | 5 (a.m.) / 5 (p.m.) | 8 | 6 | 6 | 18 | 13 | 61 |
| 7 | off | 8 | 8 | 8 | 6 | 20 | 15 | 65 |
| 8 | off | 6 | 8 | 8 | 6 | 15 | 13 | 56 |
| 9 | off | 8 | 8 | 8 | 8 | 18 | 11 | 61 |
| 10 | off | 8 | 6 | 6 | 4 | 22 | 13 | 59 |
| 11 | off | 4 (a.m.) / 4 (p.m.) | 6 | 6 | 6 | 25 | 15 | 66 |
| 12 | off | 6 | 6 | 8 | 6 | 15 | 11 | 52 |
| 13 | off | 10 | 6 | 6 | 4 | 30 | 7 | 63 |
| 14 | off | 5 (a.m.) / 5 (p.m.) | 6 | 6 | 6 | 15 | 7 | 50 |
| 15 | off | 8 | 6 | 6 | 6 | 10 | 7 | 43 |
| 16 | off | 6 | 6 | 4 | 3 | 50K! | | |

 = Fartlek　 = Hill Repeats　= Tempo　= Additional mileage day

## ULTRA TRAINING PLAN—**50 MILES TO 100K**

| WEEK | MON | TUES | WED | THURS | FRI | SAT | SUN | TOTAL |
|---|---|---|---|---|---|---|---|---|
| 1 | 6 | 6 | 4 (a.m.) / 4 (p.m.) | 6 | 4 | 15 | 9 | 54 |
| 2 | off | 6 | 8 | 8 | 4 | 17 | 9 | 52 |
| 3 | off | 8 | 5 (a.m.) / 5 (p.m.) | 6 | 6 | 20 | 11 | 61 |
| 4 | off | 8 | 8 | 4 (a.m.) / 4 (p.m.) | 8 | 15 | 11 | 58 |
| 5 | off | 8 | 8 | 5 (a.m.) / 5 (p.m.) | 8 | 20 | 15 | 69 |
| 6 | off | 5 (a.m.) / 5 (p.m.) | 8 | 6 | 6 | 18 | 15 | 63 |
| 7 | off | 8 | 8 | 8 | 6 | 22 | 15 | 67 |
| 8 | off | 6 | 4 (a.m.) / 4 (p.m.) | 8 | 6 | 25 | 13 | 66 |
| 9 | off | 8 | 4 (a.m.) / 4 (p.m.) | 8 | 8 | 20 | 15 | 57 |
| 10 | off | 8 | 6 | 6 | 4 | 25 | 20 | 69 |
| 11 | off | 8 | 6 | 6 | 6 | 15 | 15 | 56 |
| 12 | off | 6 | 6 | 8 | 6 | 25 | 25 | 76 |
| 13 | off | 5 (a.m.) / 5 (p.m.) | off | 6 | 4 | 30 | 7 | 57 |
| 14 | off | 5 (a.m.) / 5 (p.m.) | 6 | 6 | 6 | 15 | 7 | 50 |
| 15 | off | 8 | 6 | 6 | 6 | 10 | 7 | 43 |
| 16 | off | 6 | 6 | 4 | 3 | **50!** | | |

= Fartlek = Hill Repeats = Tempo = Additional mileage day

## ULTRA TRAINING PLAN—100 MILES

| WEEK | MON | TUES | WED | THURS | FRI | SAT | SUN | TOTAL |
|------|-----|------|-----|-------|-----|-----|-----|-------|
| 1 | 6 | 6 | 4 (a.m.) / 4 (p.m.) | 6 | 4 | 17 | 9 | 56 |
| 2 | off | 6 | 8 | 4 (a.m.) / 4 (p.m.) | 4 | 20 | 9 | 55 |
| 3 | off | 8 | 5 (a.m.) / 5 (p.m.) | 6 | 6 | 15 | 11 | 56 |
| 4 | off | 8 | 8 | 8 | 8 | 20 | 11 | 63 |
| 5 | off | 8 | 8 | 5 (a.m.) / 5 (p.m.) | 8 | 15 | 15 | 64 |
| 6 | off | 10 | 8 | 6 | 6 | 18 | 15 | 63 |
| 7 | off | 8 | 8 | 8 | 6 | 25 | 15 | 70 |
| 8 | off | 6 | 8 | 8 | 6 | 18 | 13 | 59 |
| 9 | off | 8 | 8 | 8 | 8 | 20 | 15 | 67 |
| 10 | off | 8 | 6 | 6 | 4 | 25 | 20 | 69 |
| 11 | off | 8 | 6 | 6 | 6 | 15 | 15 | 56 |
| 12 | off | 6 | 6 | 8 | 6 | 25 | 25 | 76 |
| 13 | off | 5 (a.m.) / 5 (p.m.) | 6 | 6 | 4 | 30 | 7 | 63 |
| 14 | off | 5 (a.m.) / 5 (p.m.) | 3 | 6 | 6 | 15 | 15 | 55 |
| 15 | off | 8 | 6 | 6 | 6 | 20 | 20 | 66 |
| 16 | off | 6 | 6 | 4 | 3 | 30 | 15 | 64 |
| 17 | off | 3 | 4 (a.m.) / 4 (p.m.) | 6 | 4 | 35 | 20 | 76 |
| 18 | off | 3 | 6 | 4 | 4 | 20 | 13 | 50 |
| 19 | off | 6 | 8 | 6 | 4 | 13 | 10 | 47 |
| 20 | 7 | 7 | 4 | 3 | 2 | 100! | | |

## TRAINING PLANS AND SETBACKS

I run at least 6 days per week. One could certainly call me obsessive if judging by the way I work to ensure that my daily run comes to fruition. A hard lesson that I had to learn over the years is that when your body is asking you for a break, whether it be expressed through sickness, lack of motivation, or injury, it is best to give in a little or risk losing a lot. You are dedicated to your training, yes, but many unforeseeable instances will be thrown your way during the course of the program. My best advice is to take setbacks in stride. Much as you won't find yourself dropping out of a 100-miler because of a lone variable, your fitness is not at risk because of a little bad luck. Keep it all in perspective.

Common variables you may bump into over the course of training include weather, illness, injury, family emergencies, work commitments, and travel. These can feel like major setbacks, leading to worry that you are going too far off plan. Let's look at instances where things are not as catastrophic for your training as they may at first seem.

Weather can be a major hindrance, although I am a firm believer that if it makes us confront our discomforts, then it is probably good training. That being said, there are times when it's just too cold, hot, or stormy to be conducive to beneficial training. Sometimes you can make the effort, but you have to ask yourself if this is going to set your training back or whether you can live with missing a day going forward with what is specified in the plan. If it is ridiculously bad outside, including air pollution, it may be a prudent move to stay indoors, opting to use a treadmill, stair climber, spin bike, rowing machine, elliptical, indoor track, or a mixture of these.

Discussing specific types of illness is beyond the scope of my expertise and certainly outside the reach of this book, so I will take a broader brush. Jumping back on schedule too soon following illness can lead to a slower recovery or cause the illness to return. It is best to make sure that you gradually move back onto your training plan after you've been sick. As I begin to turn a corner and improve, one method I adopt is to assign myself a percentage based on how close I feel to normal and then apply that to the mileage or workload in my training plan. In other words, if I feel at approximately 65 percent of my healthy self, then I will do 65 percent of the mileage called for that day. A way to gauge your percentage of recovery is to take your resting heart rate at regular intervals, say, once every couple of weeks. When you feel sick, it is likely that your heart rate will remain high, so you can look to the decrease in resting rate as a yardstick for measuring your return to health. These methods will help you fold back in the miles in a more measured, careful fashion. Although you may feel you are losing fitness with every day that passes, remember that fitness lasts for up to 2 weeks. Let's hope that your sickness does not!

Most runners eventually encounter injury of one kind or another. I had run for many years before an acute injury forced me to rethink my training and my upcoming races. I battled with plantar fasciitis for a long year, partly because I kept training through the pain. I sought treatment and worked on the symptoms, all while making a concerted effort to train and race for events as if nothing stood in my way. That only prolonged the suffering, from both a performance and a physical standpoint. I should have listened more closely to the irritations and dialed back my training, minimizing my downtime and choosing a conservative approach to getting back on schedule.

I recommend that you trust your intuition when an injury develops and seek professional help as needed. Don't let things get out of hand. Yes, downtime may be necessary, and the training plan may have to be amended before you are able to move onward with intensity, but this time off may allow for some useful crosstraining and, more important, the ability to keep your fitness and long-range plans in accordance with the time line.

And then there are the many curveballs that life throws your way. Weddings, funerals, work emergencies, travel, and other unexpected events make for excellent excuses for throwing off your training regimen. And, as with weather, illness, and injury, sometimes they do. But other times you just have to make the time. In so doing, your running may help you to cope with the stress and pressure of what may be difficult situations. Waking up at 4:00 a.m. to get in your miles while wearing a headlamp may invigorate you so that you are more capable and focused in handling a family emergency or a blowup at work. It will certainly help you sleep more soundly!

Just as the ultra for which you are training will have its many ups and downs, places where you make quick progress and sections of relentless slogging, so too will your ultra training. Keeping it all in perspective, knowing that it is all just one step toward a much larger goal, will help you to get through the rough patches. Remember why you are doing this, how you got to where you are, and that it is supposed to be fun—not all of it, perhaps, but the vast majority.

# AFTERWORD
## WHAT'S NEXT?

≡

**PARTICIPATION IN ULTRAMARATHONS IS SKYROCKETING,** with the number of entrants increasing by leaps and bounds every year. The number of races has at least doubled, maybe tripled. When I started running ultras in 1998, there were 20 or so 100-milers to choose from in a year. Now there are more than that just in the month of September alone! And many races now offer a variety of distances. That, too, is a significant change.

That the number of participants and races has made such an enormous jump says much about the intrigue of ultrarunning. And while it has created some growing pains—such as the more popular races filling up in a day, or the sometimes-frustrating lottery or point systems—for the most part, this growth has had a very positive effect on the sport.

Yes, there is a little more pomp and circumstance now, certainly with signature events such as Western States and Leadville. There is more of everything else too: media attention, runners, spectators, infrastructure. You can watch pre- and post-race interviews online, and some of the athletes are bona fide stars, with sponsors. There are also more stepping-stone races that introduce you to the trail scene, helping to feed ultra desire and interest.

Access and information are better than ever. I recall relying on a 20-word paragraph in the back of *UltraRunning* magazine to learn about an upcoming race. Doing your due diligence to prepare for a race was pretty difficult; you often had no idea what you were getting yourself into. You might know the course elevation or the route (in a bigger race). But that was about it. So you just prepared for, well, everything. Now with the click of a few buttons you can read reviews and blogs, with runners weighing in and offering cautions and recommendations. With this information you are able to dial in your training far better than was ever possible before.

There's also a little more prize money, which helps offset the costs for those training at a high level and also pushes the competition.

That said, in ultrarunning, well-regarded courses and races with heritage and history seem to carry more weight than prize money. Most people run ultras for the experience. They have not proved to be easily wooed by money. Hearing positive reviews about a course, about the people, about the aid stations—these are keys to an event's success, far more than a purse. And a hard-earned belt buckle, by most counts, is pretty priceless.

Despite rapid and exponential growth, most ultra events have successfully maintained that cherished laid-back vibe so unique to the ultra experience. If you are coming to these races from another background, perhaps experience in large marathons with thousands of participants, then you might be surprised by the ultra's unique atmosphere. Ultrarunning's allure is its grassroots feel, and along with that comes taking the time to slow down and appreciate that distinctive vibe. More than other distances, the ultra distances force you to rely more on yourself. There are fewer cheering spectators, and many times, as discussed in this book, you are entirely by yourself, for miles and hours at a time. The ultra is *not* just a marathon plus mileage. It is so much more than that.

As the sport grows, I continue to consider how I want to grow along with it. I love directing races, giving back to the sport and endeavoring to offer people an authentic ultra experience that brings them the kind of joy I have known. If putting on a top-notch event might be the thing that causes a new runner to catch the ultra bug, I am honored to have that chance to influence even one person. Through this book, at my running store, and through events I race or direct, I want to continue to share the ultrarunning ideals that I have picked up over the years, along with the most current trail and race developments, endeavoring to mix the old with the new.

Running for me is not an activity I work into my life or a pursuit with a set end point. Rather, it is an integral piece of who I am and hope to always be. It's given me a wife, child, occupation, home, community, and most of my friends that I will have for life. Even with many miles and races behind me, running an ultra still thrills me. Although I've completed my share, at every start line I am ever in awe of the task at hand, with a deep reverence and respect for the miles. The feeling usually hits me hard a little past the halfway point of a race. You are so exposed at that point, physically and mentally. There is so much behind you, yet so much ahead. It is daunting. And thrilling. An ultra forces you to put yourself out there, and it is that all-or-nothing feeling that I love. When you finally cross the finish line, the feeling of having triumphed over not just the many physical hurdles, but also the even more formidable ones of uncertainty and doubt, is like none other. I still shake my head in wonder and think, *Wow, I can't believe I just did that. Now that's a good day.*

# INDEX

# ABOUT THE **AUTHOR**

**HAL KOERNER** is the owner of Rogue Valley Runners, a specialty running store in Ashland, Oregon. As an ultramarathoner, he is one of only two people who have won both the Western States 100-Mile Endurance Run (2007, 2009) and the Hardrock 100 Endurance Run. He has also finished more than 130 ultramarathons in the United States, Europe, and Asia. He has a wife, Carly, and a daughter, Nyla, as well as two four-legged running mates, Abbey and Ember.